ÉTA[illegible]

BRITAIN'S NO[illegible]US INFANTRY BASE DEPOT (1914–1919)

ÉTAPLES

BRITAIN'S NOTORIOUS INFANTRY BASE DEPOT (1914–1919)

Stephen Wynn

First published in Great Britain in 2020 by
Pen & Sword Military
An imprint of
Pen & Sword Books Limited
Yorkshire - Philadelphia

ISBN 978 1 47384 6 036

A CIP catalogue record for this book is available from the British Library

Printed and bound in the UK
by CPI Group (UK) Ltd, Croydon, CR0 4YY

Pen & Sword Books Limited incorporates the imprints of Atlas,
Archaeology, Aviation, Discovery, Family History, Fiction, History,
Maritime, Military, Military Classics, Politics, Select, Transport, True Crime,
Air World, Frontline Publishing, Leo Cooper, Remember When, Seaforth
Publishing,
The Praetorian Press, Wharncliffe Local History, Wharncliffe Transport,
Wharncliffe True Crime and White Owl.

For a complete list of Pen & Sword titles please contact
PEN & SWORD BOOKS LIMITED
47 Church Street, Barnsley, South Yorkshire S70 2AS, United Kingdom
E-mail: enquiries@pen-and-sword.co.uk
Website: www.pen-and-sword.co.uk
Or
PEN AND SWORD BOOKS
1950 Lawrence Rd, Havertown, PA 19083, USA
E-mail: Uspen-and-sword@casematepublishers.com
Website: www.penandswordbooks.com

Contents

Introduction

Étaples-sur-mere is situated on the North Eastern coastline of France, and is part of the Pas-de-Calais, Hauts de France region.

Étaples lies on a ridge of dunes which once lay on the seaward side of an area of marshland which had formed off shore. This came about as a result of the chalk plateau off Artois, and was an area which stretched from the Canche, northwards, where the dunes tend to extend inland, all the way to the old chalk cliff.

During the First World War, this was the area chosen to set up an enormous training camp for soldiers of the British Expeditionary Force along with Allied units from other countries of the British Empire. Having completed their basic training in camps, mainly throughout the south of England, they crossed the English Channel before arriving by train at Étaples, which then became the final preparation area for Allied troops arriving in France. There they would undertake further training, which included a short course of instruction in gas warfare, and ten days of physical preparation before being deployed to front-line areas at different locations across France and Belgium. It was also the main location for British and Commonwealth soldiers returning from the Western Front, especially those who required sending back to the UK.

The camp at Étaples truly was a massive affair. It included living accommodation, training areas, military hospitals, an area for convalescence and a cemetery, which alone covers an area of some six hectares. There were parades, drills and instruction, and a training staff who became renowned for the brutality they appeared to enjoy administering upon their own troops. The gas warfare input and the ten days of training were for everyone at the camp, regardless of whether they were new recruits, experienced veterans, or the wounded who had fully recovered and were waiting to be sent back to front-line service.

The camp's hospital and medical facilities were attacked with bombs and machine guns by German aircraft on more than one occasion, several times during May 1918 alone. These raids caused death, damage and devastation. Doctors, nurses, orderlies and patients were killed and wounded during these raids.

The wife of Robert Baden-Powell, Lady Olave Baden-Powell, having arrived in France on 7 October 1915, helped staff a YMCA recreational hut at Val-de-Lievres, Calais, which had been provided by the Worshipful Company of Mercers, a renowned Livery Company of the City of London, of which Robert Baden-Powell had been the Master in 1912.

In early January 1916, Robert Baden-Powell, by then already heavily involved in the Scouting movement, arranged for another recreational hut (sponsored by the Scouts) at Étaples, which was looked after by Lady Olave and two of the other members who had started the recreational hut at Calais. Due to sickness, Lady Olave had to return home to the UK at the end of January 1916. She would later describe Étaples as 'a dirty, loathsome, smelly little town'. Maybe her description, in part, had something to do with the fact Étaples was a coastal town and was home to a large fleet of fishing trawlers. When soldiers staying at the Étaples camp were allowed out on a pass, they did not naturally gravitate towards town to find their recreational needs, preferring instead the delights on offer in the nearby town of Le Touquet, which was separated from Étaples by a small river.

Le Touquet had a pleasant beach for those of a more discerning character and, in essence, it became a place for officers only; to prevent a mass of 'fellows from the other ranks' potentially spoiling their fun, a picket guard was placed on the bridge over the river Canche, which was the only way into Le Touquet from the camp at Étaples. At low tide men were known to make their way to and from Le Touquet, by simply traversing the shallow river bed.

Men died in the camp's many hospitals, from wounds, illness and sickness, as well as German air raids, of which there were many. Some even say that the flu pandemic of 1918 began as a result of conditions at the Étaples camp.

A total of 11,434 men and women are buried at the Étaples military cemetery, who were either killed or died as result of their involvement in the First World War. Of these, 8,822 were from the United Kingdom. Another 1,143 were from Canada, 464 from Australia, 261 from New Zealand, sixty-eight from South Africa, twenty-three from India and three from Belgium; there were also 650 German graves in the cemetery as well.

The British dead included many who had been honoured with military awards for their bravery.

Major Douglas Reynolds was 31 years of age, and serving with the 37th Battery, 83rd Brigade, Royal Field Artillery, when he was involved in action which resulted in him being awarded the Victoria Cross.

The following citation for the award of his Victoria Cross appeared in the *London Gazette* newspaper on 16 November 1914.

> On 26 August 1914, at Le Cateau, France, Captain Reynolds took two teams with volunteer drivers, to recapture two British guns and limbered up two guns under heavy artillery and infantry fire. Although the enemy was within 100 yards, he managed, with the help of two drivers, Job Henry Charles Drain and Frederick Luke, to get one gun away safely.
>
> On 9 September (1914) at Pysloup, he reconnoitred at close range, discovered an (enemy) battery which was holding up the advance, and silenced it.

Privates Job Drain and Frederick Luke were also awarded the Victoria Cross for their actions alongside Reynolds that day.

Reynold's Victoria Cross was awarded to him by King George V at Buckingham Palace on 13 January 1915, having also been awarded the French award of the Cross de Chevalier de Legion d'Honneur, two months earlier on 3 November 1914.

Reynolds returned to France, and having been promoted to the rank of major, was wounded in action the result of a German gas shell attack, and subsequently died of his injuries in the Duchess of Westminster's Hospital in Le Touquet, France, on 23 February 1916.

A total of 229 men from the other ranks had been awarded the Military Medal. This included 180 who had fought with the British Army, thirty-three Canadian soldiers, twelve Australians and four from New Zealand.

There were sixty-nine officers who had been awarded the Military Cross. Of these, fifty-six were from the United Kingdom, nine were from Canada and four were from Australia.

The Meritorious Service Medal had been awarded to eleven. Of these, nine were British and the other two were from Canada.

There was a total of fifty-seven officers and men who had been Mentioned in Despatches, fifty-one from the United Kingdom, three from Canada, two from South Africa, and one from Australia.

A total of fourteen officers had been awarded the Distinguished Service Order, twelve from the United Kingdom and two from Canada.

There were a total of forty-five men who had been awarded the Distinguished Conduct Medal, of these forty were from the United Kingdom, two from Australia, two from Canada and one from South Africa.

Immediately before the war Étaples had a civilian population of around 5,000, but throughout the war and because of the military camp being its unwanted neighbour, the number of people in and around the town was more like 85,000 at any given time. In recognition of the part it played in the war, Étaples was awarded the Croix de Guerre by the French government in 1920.

Chapter One

The Étaples Mutiny 1917

Part One

The mutiny which took place at the Étaples camp in September 1917 is often looked at historically in an isolated way. By that I mean it is not looked at from a wider and connected perspective, which is very relevant to the overall topic of discussion. Looked at in isolation, it could appear quite shocking. A case of how dare the common soldier rise up against what he is told to do by his superior officers, regardless of the rights or wrongs of the situation. But I don't think it should be viewed in that way, because to do that suggests it was an isolated case, when it most definitely wasn't. Not only was it in keeping with the times, but it wasn't the first occasion that a mutiny had taken place during the First World War.

For a start, what happened at Étaples wasn't just one event, it was a number of smaller mutinies which took place throughout September 1917. Importantly, the events at Étaples were most definitely in keeping with what had happened elsewhere throughout Europe.

The first notable mutiny of the First World War, but which possibly wasn't seen in such terms at the time – or even now for that matter – was the Christmas truce of 1914. Because history has chosen to entitle the event as a 'truce', that's how it was, and still is, largely viewed to this day. But it was a mutiny, plain and simple. Let's have a look at the definition of the word 'mutiny'.

> An open rebellion against the proper authorities, especially by soldiers or sailors against their officers. (Oxford English Dictionary)

Although the Christmas truce of 1914 involved both soldiers and officers on the Western Front, it was a series of actions that was neither supported, nor approved of, by senior British military figures or the British Prime Minister and his War Cabinet; but not one British or Empire soldier was disciplined or court martialled as a result. The following Christmas, the same thing happened, albeit on a much smaller scale, but this time a court martial followed. Captain Iain Colquhoun of the Scots Guards, exchanged cigars and festive pleasantries with a German officer, during an agreed Christmas day truce where both sides stopped fighting each other and buried their dead. This was despite senior British officers having issued specific orders that there would be no repeat of the events of Christmas 1914.

Captain Colquhoun had been approached by a German officer who had walked towards the British lines, holding a white flag as his only protection, uncertain as to how the British would respond. The German officer wanted a Christmas day truce, which Colquhoun, under strict orders not to engage in such pleasantries, politely declined. He did, however, agree to a ceasefire so that the Germans could collect and bury their dead. It was during this period of time that British and German officers and soldiers chatted with each other, and exchanged cigarettes and cigars. After about an hour, a whistle was blown from the British trenches, and the ceasefire was over, but for the rest of the day neither side fired a single shot.

Ten days later Colquhoun and his men were relieved and returned to a rear-line position for some much-needed rest and recuperation. Much to his utter surprise, Colquhoun immediately found himself under arrest, and charged with conduct to the prejudice of good order and of military discipline. After a five-hour trial he was found guilty, and was punished with a reprimand, the lowest possible sentence he could receive.

That is not the full story, and it would be remiss of me not to highlight a couple of other points in this case. Besides being a captain in the British Army, he was also known as Sir Iain Colquhoun of Luss, 7th Baronet and Chief of the Clan Colquhoun. The reprimand he received at his court martial was remitted by General Sir Douglas Haig, soon after it was given. The then Prime Minister, Herbert H Asquith, was his wife's uncle, and Asquith's son, Robert Asquith, defended him at his court martial. The biggest surprise for me out of all of this was that Colquhoun was ever arrested in the first place.

Colquhoun survived the war, despite being wounded, and was awarded the Distinguished Service Order in 1916 with a Bar that followed in 1918, he was also Mentioned in Despatches.

Returning to 1917, the February revolution had taken place in Russia, which resulted in the abdication of Tsar Nicholas II on 30 February 1917, just three days after elements of the Russian Army mutinied and sided with the revolutionaries. This not only ended the Romanov dynastic rule, but also the Russian Empire. The revolution had been a long time in the making, with origins well before the start of the First World War. If anything, the outbreak of the war had simply exasperated the situation. The country was in such a dire situation that there were queues for basic items such as bread, but with the situation worsening day by day for the Russian people, the Tsar's way of dealing with the situation was to simply ignore it, hoping it would go away; it didn't.

It wasn't as though there had been no prior warning of the people's discord. February 1917 was the culmination of more than a century of unrest between a nation's down trodden people, and the Tsar and other aristocrats who kept their power only by the presence of the army. But the army had also started to become disillusioned with the Tsar, his government and senior military figures because, by January 1917, Russian casualties in the war had reached nearly 6 million, which included dead, wounded and missing. The Tsar was directly responsible for his own downfall, and this wasn't helped any in the summer of 1915 when he announced that he would personally take command of the Russian Army, against the advice of those around him. It was a disastrous decision, in part due to his lack of military tactical awareness, and because he was an extremely poor leader of men.

Word of what had happened throughout Russia had reached the ears of those in the West, including France and England. Many countries throughout Europe seemed to be in a similar position, with their societies being very class-driven, which meant there was a massive cultural and social divide separating the different sections of society, especially those individuals who were at the top and bottom of the social ladder.

Many ordinary people throughout Europe, including a large number of the young soldiers who were fighting the war, couldn't see the point of it, and had nothing personal against those they were fighting against. This was a war wanted more by politicians, senior military personnel and one or two members of some of Europe's most powerful royal families. In essence, intended or otherwise, it had become a class war.

On a slightly different note, there was also what has been called the 'Singapore Mutiny', an incident which took place on 15 February 1915. It didn't involve British soldiers mutinying, rather Indian soldiers of the 5th Light Infantry, Indian Army.

The incident happened in Singapore when some 400 sepoys who feared they were to be moved from the island to other war time duties elsewhere, mutinied. The situation lasted for a week and resulted in the deaths of eight British officers and men, two Malay officers and one soldier, fourteen British civilians, five Chinese and Malay civilians and one interned German.

The mutiny was finally put down by British forces along with Allied naval units, including some of the Imperial Japanese Navy.

It had all started on 27 January 1915, when it was announced that the men of the 5th Light Infantry, were to be transferred to Hong Kong to continue garrison duties there rather than in Singapore. Somehow, and it is not known how or why, rumours began circulating among the Indian soldiers that they were actually being redeployed to either the European theatre of war, or to Gallipoli to fight against the Turks, who, like most of them, were Muslim. Although it was nothing more than an unfounded rumour, it was enough to spark a bloody and deadly mutiny.

A farewell parade of the soldiers of the 5th Light Infantry took place on the morning of 15 February 1915, with the regiment due to sail for Hong Kong the following morning on board the commandeered troop ship, the *Nile.* Rumour control went in to overdrive, when the General

Officer Commanding Singapore failed to mention that their destination was Hong Kong.

That same afternoon, convinced they were being lied to, the mutiny took place, but not all members of the 5th Light Infantry were convinced enough to take part. In fact, only four out of the eight companies took part.

If it is the right word to use, 'luck' was on the side of the mutineers, as 15 February 1915, coincided with the Chinese New Year celebrations, which meant that nearly all the members of the local Chinese Volunteers Corps had been given periods of leave, which in effect left Singapore almost defenceless. This meant that to start with the mutineers had a free rein to do whatever they wanted to, and they took full advantage of the situation, killing some eighteen civilians, who they just happened to chance upon. Because fourteen of those who were killed were British, rumours circulated that British civilians had been intentionally targeted by the Indian troops.

The fact that more than 400 Indian troops mutinied and then went about systematically murdering British troops and civilians, strongly suggests that their mutiny was a bit more deep-rooted than believing they were being sent to Europe or Gallipoli. Their actions, I would suggest, came more out of a pent-up dislike or even hatred of the British, who had long been their masters and political rulers.

After the mutiny had been put down, a court of inquiry took place on 23 February 1915, and despite a 450 page report being compiled, the cause of the mutiny could not be conclusively established. A court martial of more than 200 Indian soldiers took place. This resulted in forty-seven of them being publicly executed outside Outram Prison, while others were sentenced to terms of imprisonment of up to twenty years.

The mutiny at Singapore is an interesting topic of discussion in its own right, and there is a lot more to it than has been included here. The only purpose of mentioning it here is as an example of the number of mutinies that took place during the course of the First World War.

What are often referred to as the 'French Army Mutinies' of May 1917 were not technically a 'mutiny', because the French soldiers did not actually refuse to fight, they simply refused to get out of their trenches and attack heavily fortified and defended German positions. They were more than willing to defend their own positions, which would always be a good thing to do when faced with an advancing enemy bearing down on you.

The French 'mutiny' was born out of frustration among the lower ranks who were fed up with being led by senior officers whose sole tactic appeared to be a suicidal, head-on frontal assault on heavily defended German positions. After suffering heavy losses during the Second Battle of the Aisne and the Nivelle Offensive, the French soldiers were left shocked, their morale was broken, and their trust and belief in General Robert Nivelle had totally evaporated. By early 1917 over one million Frenchmen had been killed, out of a total male population of just 20 million.

The French academic and military historian Guy Pedroncini, having searched the French military archives, discovered that by the end of 1917, forty-nine out of the 113 infantry divisions, had experienced some kind of rebellion or mutinous behaviour among their ranks. Throughout May 1917, the French had experienced revolts and mutinies in a total of twenty-one of their infantry divisions, as well as having to contend with 27,000 desertions.

The French authorities could neither close their eyes, nor bury their heads in the sand any longer; they finally realised change was urgently needed and Nivelle was replaced with General Philippe Petain, who quickly went about restoring his men's morale, by greatly improving their conditions and stopping the suicidal attacks on German positions. Despite all of these improvements for French soldiers, some 3,400 courts martials followed, out of which 554 death sentences were passed, although only twenty-six resulted in executions.

By the end of 1917, the British, French, Italian and South African armies had all experienced some kind of mutiny or rebellion among their troops, a lot of which was to do with class. Most soldiers came from working-class backgrounds, either on the land as farm labourers, or in one of the many new factories that had sprung up as a result of the industrial revolution. Either way, men were certainly not going to become rich by working for somebody else for a paltry wage. Those with families would more often than not struggle to keep a roof over their heads, food on the table or put clothes on their backs. Now they were fighting for their country they found themselves being led by the very men who were from the upper classes of society – men whom most of them mistrusted or disliked with a passion.

Part Two

Two interesting points to begin this part of the book with are questions that were asked in the House of Commons nearly forty years apart.

On 5 April 1978, Eric Moonman, the Labour Member of Parliament, for Basildon in Essex, asked the Secretary of State of Defence whether any papers relevant to the Haig board of inquiry in to the Étaples mutiny in 1917 were retained by the Public Record Office; if any were not accessible to public inspection; and if so, why such an exception to the normal rule had been made.

Doctor John Gilbert, the Conservative Member of Parliament for Dudley East, and the Secretary of State for Defence, replied that although the Public Record Office held a war diary for the Étaples Base (W095 Piece No. 4027), which describes the events of the mutiny, and records that a board of inquiry was set up on the spot on the authority of the commanding officer, it has not been possible to trace any papers relating either to the board of inquiry, or to one involving Field Marshal Haig. The rules governing the disposal of army records, which were still in force until recently, provided that records of inquiry need to be kept for only ten years, so it is probable that the Étaples board of inquiry records were destroyed many years ago.

On 13 April 2017, Chris Evans the Labour Member of Parliament for Islwyn in Gwent, asked the Secretary of State for Defence, whether documents relevant to the Haig Board of Inquiry in to the Étaples mutiny of 1917, had been retained by the government.

On 24 April 2017, the Secretary of State for Defence, the Right Honourable Mark Lancaster, replied that no records pertaining to the

Haig Board of Inquiry into the Étaples mutiny of 1917 had been retained by the Ministry of Defence. It is also worth noting that, on receipt of Mr Lancaster's reply, Mr Evans does not appear to have pushed him on the point.

I am absolutely staggered to discover that documentation appertaining to such an important part of Britain's history, that was entrusted to a government department, has been lost or misplaced, which I believe is highly unlikely. That being said, the only logical conclusion I can come to is that all and any such documents in relation to the Haig Board of Inquiry were intentionally destroyed, on the direction or instruction of an unknown individual, or individuals, in such a position of power that they would have the relevant authority to make such a decision.

The Étaples base was nominated as the No. 2 Training Camp, which included 'Gas Areas', before being sent to the front lines of the Western Front on active service. Men who had endured active service and been wounded would often find themselves back at Étaples being treated in one of the camp's numerous medical facilities. There was the St John Hospital, the No. 1 Canadian General Hospital, the No. 26 General Hospital, the No. 51 General Hospital, the No. 7 Canadian General Hospital, the No. 1 General Hospital for officers, No. 24 General Hospital, No. 56 General Hospital, No. 46 Stationary Hospital, and No. 6 Convalescent Camp.

It was also used as a temporary base by men who were being transferred to other theatres of war, those who were waiting to be sent home after receiving hospital treatment and a period of convalescence. There were also those men who had returned from the front line and were waiting to be transferred to other units after their original one had been greatly depleted.

It has to be remembered that this was an enormous camp which included a Women's Hostel (which in the main catered for nursing staff), a Detention Centre, a headquarters for the British Red Cross, an Army Service Corps depot, a Royal Engineers camp, numerous accommodation blocks for different Labour Corps units, and Infantry Base Depots for

British, Canadian and New Zealand troops. The camp was something of a strange affair as it also incorporated large training areas, part of which was referred to by the men as the 'Bull Ring', which allowed for tactical infantry training, live-firing as well as gas attacks.

Although there were men of all different levels of experience, while at the camp they were all treated the same by the training staff, which did not go down at all well. It mattered not to them if a man was a brand-new recruit on his way to the front, or an experienced soldier on his way back; they were all expected to do exactly the same, which to most seemed a ridiculous scenario and a complete waste of time. But the edict of the day from the perspective of the training staff appeared to be that discipline is discipline and orders are orders, no matter who you are. This attitude was not at all appreciated by those who had already served at the front. They had done soldiering for real. They had killed the enemy and seen their friends and colleagues killed by bullets and bombs alike, none of which had been a pleasant experience, and once back at the Étaples camp, they were treated as harshly as raw recruits. To these men it made absolutely no sense. What made matters even more unpalatable for them was that many, if not all, of those administering the training had never seen action on the Western Front – or anywhere else for that matter. The only knowledge they possessed of military tactics had been gleamed from a service manual. Ultimately, all this led to was resentment of the training staff. The men's cooperation on the matter was not helped any by their treatment, and the conditions they were expected to endure while there.

Étaples was one of the biggest and most well established camps throughout France, but most of the men who spent time there found their accommodation was nothing more substantial than a tent, no matter what the weather was like. The food they were provided with was not what one might expect, with some describing it as being no better than what they would eat in the trenches.

The best way of describing just how bad the conditions and the regime were perceived to be came in the shape of a report, in which it had been noted that it was not uncommon for men who were quite clearly still recovering from their wounds, to return to serve with their units on the 'front lines', rather than stay a day longer than they had to at the camp.

So poisonous was the atmosphere that was a part of everyday life at Étaples, that when taking into account the prevailing mutinous and rebellious events that had, and were still, taking place elsewhere in Europe, it was obvious that it wouldn't take too much more to tip the balance to breaking point at the camp. So strict was the regime that the slightest infringement of any of the rules or instructions put in place by the instructors was dealt with in the severest of ways.

Although the pleasant French seaside town of Le Touquet, where a man could find most, if not all, of the pleasantries that he sought, was no more than a stone's throw away from the camp, it was off limits to enlisted men. A man had more chance of been shot dead by a German bullet than he did obtaining a 'pass in to town'.

The issue about men from the other ranks not being allowed in to Le Touquet, because it was for officers only, went some way to highlighting the social issues which existed at that time, between the 'haves' and the 'have nots'. Not even a war was going to change that.

Two of the First World War's most respected poet-soldiers, Wilfred Owen and Siegfried Sassoon, both wrote about their own experiences of Étaples.

Wilfred Owen enlisted in the Artists Rifles Officers' Training Corps, and after completing his basic training on 4 June 1916, he was commissioned as a Second Lieutenant in the Manchester Regiment. As a result of being involved in fighting on the Western Front, Owen was diagnosed with neurasthenia, which was more commonly known as shell shock, and sent for treatment at Craiglockhart War Hospital in Edinburgh. Between 1916 and 1919 it was used as a military psychiatric hospital for shell-shocked officers. It was while recuperating at Craiglockhart that he met fellow soldier poet, Siegfried Sassoon.

Owen returned to active service in France in July 1918, and by the end of August, he was back in the front line serving with the 2nd Battalion, Manchester Regiment. As a result of his actions in storming a number of German strongholds near the village of Joncourt on 1 October 1918,

Owen was awarded the Military Cross. The citation of his award was worded as follows:

> 2nd Lieutenant, Wilfred Edward Salter Owen, 5th Bn. Manch. R., T.F., attd. 2nd Bn. For conspicuous gallantry and devotion to duty in the attack on the Fonsomme Line on October 1st/2nd, 1918. On the company commander becoming a casualty, he assumed command and showed fine leadership and resisted a heavy counter-attack. He personally manipulated a captured enemy machine gun from an isolated position and inflicted considerable losses on the enemy. Throughout he behaved most gallantly.

Just one week before the Armistice was signed, Owen was killed in action during the crossing of the Sambre-Oise Canal; he was promoted to the rank of Lieutenant on 5 November 1918, the day after his death. His mother received a telegram informing her of his death after the announcement and celebrations of the end of the war. Of the mutiny at Étaples, Owen wrote:

> I thought of the very strange look on all their faces in that camp; an incomprehensible look, which a man will never see in England; nor can it be seen in any battle, but only in Étaples. It was not despair, or terror, it was more terrible than terror, for it was a blindfold look and without expression, like a dead rabbit's.

Part Three

Now I want to consider the actual Étaples mutiny itself. As already mentioned, documents from the Haig Inquiry into the mutiny mysteriously disappeared, when or how, nobody really knows. The events of the mutiny were recorded in the camp diary, which did survive, and can be found at the Public Record Office. As a factual historical document it is questionable as to how unbiased it would be, as understandably it is not going to include anything that could possibly be interpreted as being detrimental to, or against the good name and character of the British authorities.

The Étaples Mutiny, as it is referred to, is in essence a sequence of events which took place throughout September 1917, but another incident had taken place at Étaples a year earlier on 28 August 1916, which was potentially just as explosive.

Private 3254 Alexander Little, of the 10th Battalion, Australian Imperial Force, was being taken to the punishment and detention compound within the Étaples camp, after he had verbally abused a British non-commissioned officer by telling him to 'Go fuck yourself.' The reason for the outburst had been due to his frustration after the water he was showering in was suddenly cut off without warning. Little was not happy at his treatment and began struggling to get away from his escort. He was helped in his endeavours by other members of the Australian Imperial Force, as well as soldiers from the New Zealand Expeditionary Force. The British authorities did not treat this incident lightly, and after investigating it further, they managed to identify four of these men, including Little, who were tried before a court martial, found guilty of mutiny, and sentenced to death. Three of the men had their sentences commuted to terms of detention. I am assuming that these three men were New Zealanders, because Australian authorities did not permit soldiers of the Australian Imperial Force to face the prospect of capital punishment. Alexander Little's stay of execution did not see him survive the war; he was killed in action on 4 June 1918. He has no known grave, but his name is commemorated on the Villers-Bretonneux Memorial, which is situated in the Somme region of France.

The one man who was involved in the incident who was not so fortunate, was Private 24/1521 Jack Braithwaite 2nd Battalion, Otago Regiment, of the New Zealand Expeditionary Force. He was born in Dunedin in 1885, to Joseph and Mary-Ann Braithwaite, Joseph earned his living as the proprietor of a book shop in Dunedin. Jack volunteered for the New Zealand Expeditionary Force in May 1915, a matter of months after his younger brother, Horace, also a Private (8/813), had been severely wounded serving at Gallipoli, while also a member of the Otago, Regiment. Sadly, Horace died as a result of his wounds on 15 January 1916, when he was 30 years of age.

After having completed his basic training in New Zealand, Jack Braithwaite was sent to Egypt, where he arrived in early February 1916, and was posted to the 2nd Battalion, Otago Regiment. But he was only there a couple of months before being sent to France, where he arrived in late April 1916.

It would appear that it was only after having arrived in France, having been promoted to the rank of lance corporal just prior to leaving Egypt, that his discipline record started to become somewhat erratic. Not long after arriving in France he was demoted to private after going absent without leave. This act of ill-discipline saw him appear before a New Zealand Field General Court Martial, and resulted in him facing three charges; for being absent without leave, making a false statement to an officer, and for using another man's leave pass. He was found guilty on all three charges, and his collective punishment was sixty days of No. 2 Field Punishment, which meant that he was placed in fetters and handcuffs, but unlike in the case of a No. 1 Field Punishment, he was not attached to a fixed object. He could also be liable to hard labour and a loss of pay.

The incident which ultimately resulted in Braithwaite being put before a firing squad simply does not add up, and I can therefore only sensibly conclude that his sentence was carried out to set an example to other men serving with the New Zealand Expeditionary Force, as well as those serving with the Australian forces.

On the day of Private Little's altercation with a British Military Policeman, Braithwaite was acting as a mess orderly and during the commotion he led Little to his tent, he said to try and calm the situation down. This act of conciliation was interpreted by the British authorities as an act of mutiny, with him being one of the main offenders. Along with Little and two other Australians, Braithwaite was put before a Court Martial on 11 October 1916, found guilty and sentenced to death.

His death sentence was not commuted, instead it was confirmed by General Sir Douglas Haig, the Commander-in-Chief of the British Expeditionary Force. The reason given for his execution going ahead was that he was a repeat offender, but as I have already said, I do not believe that was the real reason he received the punishment that he did.

He was executed by a twelve-man firing squad on the morning of 29 October 1916, and was buried at the Saint Sever Cemetery Extension which is situated on the outskirts of Rouen, in the Seine-Maritime region of France.

The 10th Battalion, Australian Imperial Force, was part of the 3rd Infantry Brigade, who had landed at Gallipoli on Saturday 24 April 1915. They remained there until late December 1915, when they were evacuated to Egypt, and in March 1916, they sailed for France and the Western Front. In June 1918, they were involved in fighting near Merris, in the Hauts-de-France region of the country. The men of the 10th Battalion were brave men. By the end of the war 2,136 of them had been wounded and 1,015 of them killed. There had been forty-seven occasions when men of the 10th Battalion had been mentioned in despatches. Nine men were awarded the Meritorious Service Medal, 149 men awarded the Military Medal, of which eleven received a bar, and one man received a second bar. There were thirty-four Military Crosses awarded, of which four men received a bar. The Distinguished Conduct Medal was awarded to men of the battalion on sixteen occasions. There were nine awards of the Distinguished Service Order, with one man receiving a bar. One award of the Conspicuous Medal of Gallantry, with the Victoria Cross being awarded to three members of the battalion.

So it is clear that more than a year before the Étaples Mutiny, not everything had been as it should have been at the camp. More than a year later there were still problems at the camp, so I can only assume that lessons had not been learned, and the behaviour of the staff had most definitely not changed.

The man whom history has credited with being ultimately responsible for the start of the Étaples Mutiny is Gunner Arthur Healy, known more commonly by his nickname of 'Jock'. Healy was a Gunner in the

New Zealand Army, which was part of No. 27 Infantry Base Depot, which was part of the New Zealand section of the camp.

At low tide on Sunday 9 September 1917, Healy and a few of his colleagues began walking across the estuary which separated the Étaples camp from Le Touquet. They did so to ensure that they did not have to pass the picket of Military Police officers who stood guard on the bridge, making sure that nobody crossed over it who wasn't supposed to.

The problem for Gunner Healy was that after having made his way to Le Touquet and spent a period of recreation there, it was time to get back to camp. But when he went to make his way back across the estuary, he discovered to his horror that the tide had come in, blocking his preferred way back and leaving him with no alternative but to return to the camp via the bridge. He would have known he was going to be stopped on the bridge by the Military Police officers, or the 'red caps', as they were usually referred to by the soldiers. As Healy made his way across the bridge he was, as expected, stopped and detained. What might have surprised him, however, was being detained as a deserter, which he clearly was not.

The fact he had left the camp without a pass meant detention by the Military Police was the price he had to pay; it was what followed that needs dissecting to fully understand what the mutiny at Étaples was all about. Was the behaviour of the Military Police in keeping with how they generally operated at that time? Was the reaction of the Australian and New Zealand soldiers a reflection of how they felt about the treatment of Healy by the Military Police, or was it something much deeper? Was it a colonial issue, whereby they believed the British Military Police viewed the ANZACs as inferior to them, as second-class citizens? Perhaps the Military Police treatment of Healy was the straw that finally broke the camel's back.

The reaction to the treatment of Healy might well have been the belated and sub-conscious response to the 'Little' incident, which resulted in the execution of Braithwaite. Compare this to British-held military attitudes of the time, where strict discipline was all important, and a man's life did not count for much in the eyes of some senior British officers, especially if it could be used to set an example to others, or as a stick to beat people with. These same officers saw Australian and New Zealand soldiers as generally being ill-disciplined and not up to the same high standards of which they believed all British soldiers were in possession. It was a crazy situation, not helped by the many other mutinous and rebellious acts that had already been witnessed by all sides, especially throughout 1917.

Sections of the upper echelons of British society, which included the officer class of the British Army, were concerned, worried and deeply suspicious of the common man and of where such mutinous and rebellious behaviour was going to end. For many, there was a belief that once the war was over everything was simply going to return to how it had been before. The only ones who didn't seem to understand that wasn't going to be the case, were them. Maybe that's where the real origins of the mutiny at Étaples came from.

On his detention by the Military Police, Healy was taken to a nearby detention centre where he was locked up. News of his arrest and detention quickly reached his colleagues back in the New Zealand section of the camp. A large group of angry and disgruntled officers and men quickly gathered and, ready for a confrontation, they promptly set off towards the detention centre.

Possibly the Military Police realised what kind of reaction Healy's arrest was likely to have among his colleagues, or maybe because they had heard of the large angry mob of New Zealanders on their way to the detention centre, but either way, they released Healy. It would appear that the gesture was too little too late, and matters had simply gone too far for it to all go away by somebody just saying 'sorry'. As the saying goes, it was the 'straw that broke the camel's back', which was not helped any when a large number of Military Police turned up to support their colleagues and try and disperse the crowd of New Zealanders. The two groups began shouting and swearing at each other, and before long the confrontation became physical. Sadly, it did not stop there. A shot rang out, with the noise quickly gaining everybody's attention. Maybe out of a combination of fear, panic and inexperience, one of the Military Policemen opened fire on the crowd. The errant rounds fired from Private 7683963 H Reeve's revolver struck two unsuspecting victims: a soldier,

21-year-old Corporal 240120 W.B. Wood of the 1st/4th Battalion, Gordon Highlanders, who was killed, and an unnamed French female civilian.

Corporal Wood was subsequently buried at the Étaples Military Cemetery, situated within the camp. The headstone on his grave is engraved with the inscription, 'Asleep in Jesus Till the Day Dawn and the Shadows Flee Away.' His parents, John and Rebecca Wood, lived at 10 Mid Street, Rosehearty, Aberdeenshire, Scotland. It is not clear if they were informed of the actual circumstances leading to his death.

The Military Police officers, especially Private Reeve, understood that their lives were now in imminent danger, and that they needed to get themselves to safety as quickly as they could. If any or all of them had been captured by the crowd, the chances are that they would not have survived long in such a hostile environment. It is fair to say that if the Military Police had not taken themselves out of the affray, many more people would have died that day, on both sides.

As news of the shooting spread, so more men from the camp gathered. Bad as the situation was, it had become a whole lot worse with the shooting of Corporal Wood, because now it wasn't only the New Zealander and Australian contingents who were angry, but also the naturally aggressive Scottish soldiers. By 7.30 pm the crowd of angry soldiers had risen to well over 1,000 men, which meant that the situation for the rest of the Military Police in Étaples camp had become somewhat precarious to say the least. They beat a hasty retreat to the relative safety of Étaples town.

The level of ill-feeling towards the Military Police hadn't changed any the following day, Monday 10 September 1917, and many of the soldiers, especially those who served with Gunner Healy and Corporal Wood, understandably wanted answers. The situation was deemed to be serious enough for a senior British Army officer and a high ranking member of the Military Police to pay a 'flying' visit to Étaples to see for themselves what the actual situation was. The two men were Major-General Joseph John Asser, the General Officer Commanding, Lines of Communications, British Troops in France, who was accompanied by Major Dugdale from the Corps of the Military Police General Headquarters.

Despite the level of unrest at Étaples and the 'stand-off' between the enraged troops and the Military Police, it took the camp commandant, Brigadier Thomson, until Tuesday 11 September 1917 to officially ask for reinforcements to help deal with the worsening situation. By that time he had gradually began to lose control of the situation. On Wednesday 12 September 1917, he had given an order confining all officers and soldiers to Étaples camp, but the order had virtually no authority. It was nothing more than wishful thinking, or a forlorn hope blowing perilously in the wind; as if to prove this point, more than 1,000 men broke out of the camp and marched on the town of Étaples, before making their way back to camp later the same day. One would imagine that the reason no attempt was made to detain any of them was because of their numbers, in comparison to the number of available pickets.

With the situation having reached a critical stage, urgent action was required by the British military authorities, a feeling no doubt endorsed by the Prime Minister and the British government. No one in authority was prepared to run the risk of a full-scale mutiny taking place at Étaples, because of the long-term damage it would do to military morale, and the possibility that it would be copied by other British units.

Late on the afternoon of Wednesday 12 September 1917, re-enforcements finally arrived to help the camp commandant and his beleaguered Military Police regain full control of the Étaples camp. This came in the form of 400 officers and men of the Honourable Artillery Company who, besides their firearms, had been armed with large wooden staves, ready for action, in no matter what form it might manifest itself. Having looked at the website of the Honourable Artillery Company, I could find no mention of their involvement in the Étaples mutiny.

During the first few days of the mutiny there are a number of reports that talk about ad-hoc meetings having taken place between some of the mutineers and officers, either from the Étaples camp, or to do with the Corps of Military Police. I can only assume that at these meetings, representatives of the mutineers had a list of demands, and questions they wanted answering before matters could go back to normal. The problem with this suggestion is that no official written records of any such meetings were ever made. If they were, they certainly did not survive, although many years after the war, accounts from men who were at Étaples did come to light that helped shed some light on what happened during the time of the mutiny.

One aspect of the mutiny which doesn't get too much attention is that of the deserters. These were men who at one time or another had been stationed at the camp, and due to a combination of their treatment and the conditions in which they were expected to live, had decided that desertion from the British Army was preferable, and a better existence than being a soldier at the camp.

The Monocled Mutineer, written by William Allison and John Fairley, includes the time and events of the Étaples Mutiny. Part of the book comprises first-hand accounts from some of those individuals who were at Étaples camp during the mutiny. As all of the statements and other documents from the Haig inquiry into the mutiny were subsequently and inexcusably lost, these accounts help provide some clarity to the events that took place of September 1917; they also provide a narrative other than that recorded in the camp's wartime diaries.

One of the individuals quoted in the book was a Private Phil Chester of the Northumberland Fusiliers, who told Allison and Fairley:

> The moment you got to the Bullring [the camp's training area] the routine was you fell out and sat on the sand until the instructors came. This particular morning when they told us to get up, nobody moved. We just kept sitting. It was truly an amazing sight to look around and see thousands and thousands of men just sitting there silently. There were sergeant-majors, corporals and instructors by the hundreds, all shouting at us to get to our feet. Not a man moved. In the end, they got us up by promising us we could go back to camp and have a day's rest.

Just that one act of defiance must have been quite monumental for both sides, and one that I would imagine would have had a more worrying effect on the instructors than it did the men. What must they have thought? What must have been going through their heads? Greatly outnumbered, up against thousands upon thousands of men who were showing no aggression, no violence, but were simply being silent. That must have been a somewhat unnerving experience, a shift in the power between the instructors and the men, which both sides would have immediately realised.

> Back at the camp, the sit down troops were given a meal, and when they had finished eating they were asked, 'Any complaints?' Phil Chester and his mates were so astonished that they celebrated by bursting through the railway-bridge pickets into Étaples.
>
> The mutineers who had not returned to the base on the Sunday night, had instinctively had their way to link up with the permanent deserters who flourished in the woods around Paris Plage, most of them under the patronage and guidance of Percy Toplis.

Another ex-soldier mentioned in the book was William Stephens. He also spoke about Toplis, which is an interesting aspect of the Étaples mutiny, because in certain quarters it is claimed that Toplis was never at Étaples and that at the time of the mutiny, he was actually on his way to India with his unit. I will explore this point elsewhere in the book when I look at Toplis in more detail.

> Mr William Stephens of Elsynge, was also at Paris Plage when the mutineers and the deserters joined forces on the Monday. He remembered seeing Toplis's name on wanted posters in the area.
>
> 'If he was a villain then he was not the only one around Étaples. Maybe he too, was tired of being humiliated,

> deprived, brutalised and treated like a dog. We had all got tired of being treated with less consideration than that given to horses.'
>
> It was a strange council of war which convened on the morning of Monday. The clear headed Toplis, fresh from an overnight stay at the Hotel des Anglais, where he had posed as an officer just back from the front line on leave, had to do most of the thinking for them.
>
> The delight of the deserters was boundless when they heard that the military police were no more. They were eager to show their gratitude, and assured that the coast had quite literally cleared, they offered to return to Étaples with the mutineers to take part in day two of the mutiny, under Toplis's leadership.
>
> This weird mixed bag of disaffection and desertion started marching on Étaples in the later afternoon. They were about 1,000 strong and they swung along the coast road. Before they got to the Canche bridge, they merged and then split up into four separate groups, each numbering over two hundred.
>
> Toplis felt he had a clear duty. He headed his mob straight for the detention compound and released the prisoners, about fifty of them.

Also mentioned in *The Monocled Mutineer* was a French civilian, Madame Andree Dissous, who was a resident of Étaples. She explains, 'I saw 200 or so men just march up to the compound gates, issue some threats, and the next thing, the prisoners with their shaven heads, came tumbling through the gates.'

Private (46532) George Souter of the Lancashire Fusiliers, who had previously been a private (MS/1359) in the Army Service Corps and had first arrived in France on 5 October 1914, gives an account of an incident involving Brigadier Thomson, who was driving through the camp in his car, and Toplis who was manning a road block that had been erected by the mutineers.

> Thomson stood up in the back, only to have his opening sentence drowned in a storm of abuse. He got as far as, 'How dare you call yourself soldiers, British soldiers,' when the mob closed in on his vehicle and started to rock it violently. He was forced to sit down again.
>
> Toplis had dressed for his part. That is to say, this was one of the few occasions when he was actually attired in a private's uniform and not that of an officer. He held up his hand, signalling for silence from his followers. What a sight it was to see the commanding officer there with tears in his eyes, begging us to let this trouble subside, and appealing for us to keep up the tradition of the British Army.
>
> The sight of the ashen-faced general, sitting now in the back seat, encouraged Toplis to climb on the running-board and dictate the terms for the end of the mutiny. The revolt would end he told Thomson, only when the town of Étaples was thrown open to the troops, when the Bullring had been closed, the military police removed and food and general conditions improved.

A couple of points worth mentioning here. In the days and weeks immediately after the mutiny, it is estimated that some 10,000 troops who were at Étaples during that time, and regardless of whether they were directly or indirectly involved, were moved out of the camp and towards the Western Front and the Battle of Passchendaele, or The Third Battle of Ypres, as it was also called. This battle had begun on 31 July 1917 and continued until 10 November 1917.

Many of these men would have undoubtedly been wounded or killed at Passchendaele. The Commonwealth War Graves Commission website records that between 20 September and 10 November 1917, 32,488 British soldiers, eight Australian soldiers, and 2,061 New Zealand soldiers, were killed while serving and fighting in Belgium.

The other point worth mentioning is that on Saturday 15 September 1917, the majority of those in the camp moved out, and an equally large number of new recruits arrived for their first experience of life at Étaples. The changes that the mutineers had fought for, some at the cost of their freedom and their lives, were immediately put in to place. This meant that the men had the freedom to go in to Étaples town, or bathe in the sea. The ludicrous and somewhat pointless training at the 'Bullring' was immediately dispensed with. For those who had already been through the Étaples camp, it was too little too late, but their sacrifices had not been in vain, and at least those responsible for the running of the camp had realised that urgent changes needed to be made, if there was not to be a repetition. Despite these improvements there were further 'disturbances' at Étaples until the end of the war and beyond.

A good question is why were members of the Honourable Artillery Company sent to quell the embers of a mutiny involving thousands of their comrades? How could the authorities who were sending them be absolutely certain that they would do what they were supposed to do, and not simply take up with the disgruntled soldiers in the camp? Many of those being sent were officer cadets, or those who had been identified as being officer material. The Honourable Artillery Company were assisted in successfully putting down the mutiny at Étaples by a detachment from the Machine Guns Corps, who were armed with an array of weapons including several Vickers machine guns, which were water-cooled machine guns which fired a standard .303 bullet at up to 500 rounds per minute.

If matters had escalated and the Honourable Artillery Company had been deployed against those who had taken part in the mutiny, the military authorities had in reserve two battalions of infantry from the 7th Division along with elements of cavalry of the 15th and 19th Hussars.

How members of these units would have actually felt about fighting against their own men is unclear, but it would have not been an easy scenario to deal with for anybody involved.

On Thursday 13 September 1917, the members of the Honourable Artillery Company, were ready and in place to deal with any further disturbances by the incumbent troops at the Étaples camp. When the unrest finally came to an end, some 300 of those who had been directly involved in the troubles were arrested, but thankfully for all concerned there was no more violence. Some of those detained were charged with a number of military offences. Five of these were not even 'men' in the truest sense, they were just boys aged between 17 and 19 years of age, but they were still sentenced to ten years imprisonment.

One of those who was charged was 30-year-old Lance Corporal 26/626 Jesse Robert Short, who served with the 24th (Tyneside Irish) Battalion, Northumberland Fusiliers. He was a married man who, before the war, had lived at 11 Parkinson Street, Felling, County Durham, with his wife Dinah.

He was charged before a court martial with the offence of 'Attempted Mutiny', in that he encouraged his men to put down their weapons and carry out an attack on 26-year-old Captain Eric Fitzwater Wilkinson, MC, MiD, of 'A' Company, 8th Battalion, West Yorkshire Regiment (Prince of Wales Own). Lance Corporal Short was found guilty as charged, and the sentence passed down on him was death by firing squad; his execution took place on 4 October 1917 at Boulogne. He is buried at the Boulogne Eastern Cemetery, which is situated in the Pas de Calais region of France. The inscription on his grave stone, reads: 'Duty called and he went forward ever remembered by his wife and children.'

The English folk rock band, The Levellers, wrote about the life of Corporal Short on a track of their second Album, *Static on the Airwaves*, that was released on 25 June 2012. The name of the track was, 'Mutiny'.

Three other soldiers also faced courts martial and were each sentenced to ten years imprisonment. A further ten soldiers were jailed for a year with hard labour, thirty-three men received sentences of between seven and ninety days field punishments, and a number of others were either fined or reduced in rank.

As for Captain Wilkinson, he was one of a number of British Army officers who would later become famous as having been remembered as a wartime poet. Before the war he had lived with his parents, Herbert and Mary Wilkinson, at 'Nethergrove' Portesham, Weymouth, Dorset. Previously wounded on three separate occasions, including being gassed, he was killed in action on 9 October 1917, his death came just five days after Short had been executed by firing squad. He has no known grave, but his name is commemorated on the Tyne Cot Memorial, which is situated in the West-Vlaanderen, Belgium.

Chapter Two

Victor Grayson

Albert Victor Grayson, who was often referred to by his middle name of 'Victor,' was a very interesting character in relation to the events at Étaples in September 1917.

He was born in Liverpool on 5 August 1881 to William and Elizabeth Grayson. His father was a staunch Yorkshireman as well a successful carpenter throughout the Bootle area.

On leaving school, Victor had two main interests: engineering, for which he obtained an apprenticeship, and politics, joining the Independent Labour Party. Despite having a noticeable stammer, he was noted as being an excellent orator, who certainly knew how to hold a crowd, which he managed to do with consummate ease during many of the lectures he gave, often to very big crowds.

When he was just 25 years of age, which was extremely young in a political sense, he stood as a candidate for the Independent Labour Party in the 1907 Colne Valley by-election after being nominated by the Colne Valley Labour League. Despite his age he won the seat, but only by a narrow margin, which was seen at the time as being an incredible victory. His time as a Member of Parliament was relatively short lived as he lost his seat at the 1910 General Election. So poor was his following that he lost his deposit, but he persevered with politics by continuing with his lectures at numerous locations up and down the country. It was around this time that he had begun drinking heavily and in 1913, he suffered a mental breakdown.

Such was Grayson's prominence as a socialist that Lenin, the future head of the government of the Soviet Union, wrote about him in Pravda that he was 'a very fiery socialist, but one not strong in principles and given to phrase-mongering'. Not that his piece contained too much in the way of a positive endorsement for the Liverpudian.

Grayson, who had suffered a mental breakdown in 1913, had surprised and shocked his left-wing colleagues by openly supporting Britain's entry in to the war in August 1914, even conducting recruitment drives to encourage young men to join up and enlist in the army. Grayson even went as far as enlisting in the army himself. Having travelled to New Zealand he became a soldier in the New Zealand Army on 28 November 1916, when he was then posted the 12th Company, 1st Battalion, Canterbury Regiment. After having completed his basic training in New Zealand, he set sail for England, leaving from Wellington on 26 April 1917, before arriving at Devonport in England on 20 July 1917, a journey of some three months. The reasons for this seemingly odd move are unknown. After a further two months of training in England, he left for France on 5 September 1917, and on 9 September, along with his New Zealand colleagues, he marched in to Étaples camp just around the time of the riots, disorder and mutiny. After a two-week stay at the camp he underwent additional training in preparation for being despatched to the Western Front, arriving there on 16 September. On 12 October, nearly a month after arriving, he was wounded in action and tended to by No. 1 New Zealand Field Ambulance, before being sent to No. 17 Casualty Clearing Centre later the same day. Two days later he was sent to No. 9 General Hospital at Rouen, but his wounds were thought to be severe enough that, two days later, it was necessary to repatriate him to England by Hospital Ship, where he ended up at the No. 1 New Zealand General Hospital, at Brockenhurst, Hampshire.

Grayson stayed loyal to his political views after the war, in a world where there were still growing concerns about revolutions, especially among politicians and the elite of British society. Even before the end of the war Grayson had come to the attention of Special Branch on account of his left-wing views. Sir Basil Thomson was the man in charge of the 'secretive' unit, which had originally been set up in March 1883, to combat the rise of the Irish Republican Brotherhood, whose vision was that of an independent democratic republic in Ireland. Sir Basil was concerned about

Grayson in a political sense, not solely because of his left-wing views, but also suspicions that he was working for both the Russian government and had connections with the Irish Republican Army.

Sir Basil tasked Arthur John Maundy Gregory, more commonly known as Maundy Gregory, to spy on Grayson. Gregory was, besides other things, known to be a 'political fixer'. His real claim to fame was being involved in a scandal surrounding the selling of honours by the then Prime Minister, David Lloyd George, for between £10,000 and £40,000, depending on which 'honour' was being sought.

Grayson discovered that Gregory was spying on him. He also found out about the 'honours scandal' and who was involved in it, and made reference to it at a public meeting in Liverpool, saying he would name names. Now that is not necessarily a positive strategy to undertake against someone of such high political office and social standing.

On 28 September 1920, Grayson was out socialising in London with some friends when he received a phone call. On returning to the group he informed them that he had to leave them for a while, but that he would soon return so that they could continue with their night out. Oddly enough, he made a point of saying that he had to go to the Queen's Hotel in London's Leicester Square. That was the last time that Grayson was ever seen alive. What happened to him? Nobody knows for sure, although there has been much speculation about what did happen to him and why. The theories vary and include him being murdered to shut him up over the honours scandal; that it had something to do with Étaples; that he was part of a spy ring so he vanished, changed his identity and carried on living a normal life elsewhere under a different name; and even that he had simply enough of the life that he was living. Whatever the truth, Gregory was believed to be involved in the matter to some degree.

All these years later, the likelihood of uncovering any new information or evidence that can shed light on what happen at Étaples is highly unlikely. Finding out anything about the disappearance of Grayson is even less likely. But sometimes that is what history does to us. It does not provide us with a definitive answer, it simply leaves us with ifs, buts and maybes.

Chapter Three

Regiments Used or Considered in Putting Down the Mutiny

The 1st Battalion, Honourable Artillery Company, the 1st Battalion, Royal Welsh Fusiliers, and the 22nd Battalion, Manchester Regiment, who were both part of the 7th Division, became involved in the Étaples Mutiny by being the three battalions sent to the camp by General Headquarters, just in case matters worsened and events escalated out of control. Two other units, both cavalry sections, the 15th and 19th Hussars, were held in reserve, but were not actually deployed to Étaples.

The first to arrive at Étaples were the 400 officers and men of the Honourable Artillery Company, on the evening of Wednesday 12 September 1917. They were deployed in their entirety the following morning, but in a defensive capacity and as a show of force so that those soldiers from the camp who were involved in the mutiny would give up their dissent and rebellious behaviour, which to a large degree they did.

The 1st Battalion, Honourable Artillery Company, had been in France since September 1914, and proceeded to take part in the 1st Battle of Ypres, in the later months of 1914. They also took part in the Battle of Ancre in 1916, and the Battle of Arras in 1917. They had been specifically selected for sending to Étaples as it was felt that as an officer training battalion, they would be less likely to side with the common, rebellious soldiers they were being sent to suppress.

In October 1917, Second-Lieutenant C.J. Corbett, of the Honourable Artillery Company, and a well-known cricketer and international hockey player, was in hospital at Étaples suffering from a severe wound to his right thigh. There was no explanation about what type of wound it was or how he had sustained it. I wonder if he was one of those members of the Honourable Artillery Company, who had been sent to help deal with the mutiny at the camp, the previous month.

The Royal Welch Fusiliers arrived at just before midnight on Thursday 13 September 1917, while the Manchesters arrived early the following morning, about three hours before sunrise. Later that afternoon, one company of men of the Fusiliers was deployed to protect the camp's detention block; other than that the rest of the Fusiliers and the Manchesters remained ready, but in their respective camps, just in case they too needed to be deployed.

When both battalions were told they were going to Étaples, I wonder if they were informed of the reason why? If they were, did it make any difference to how they conducted themselves when they arrived?

The 22nd Battalion, Manchester Regiment, was a service battalion and was also known as the 7th City Pals Battalion. They had been raised by the Lord Mayor of Manchester in conjunction with the city's major cotton producers on 21 November 1914. But by the time of the mutiny at Étaples, they were battle-hardened troops, having seen action at the French village of Mametz, in June 1916, where sixty members of 'A' Company came face-to-face with German forces who had held the village from early in the war. Although it was a successful confrontation for the Manchesters, they suffered a number of casualties, 198 of whom were killed.

On the first day of the Battle of the Somme, the 22nd Manchesters, as part of the 7th Division, were tasked with a first objective of taking what had been given the name of 'Bucket Trench'. After successfully completing their task they moved on to 'Danzig Alley', but were somewhat taken by surprise to find that the German defenders had not been killed during the previous week's artillery bombardment as they were expecting; they had simply held out in their underground bunkers and came out when the bombardment had stopped. With support from the South Staffordshire Regiment, the Manchesters finally took their second objective of the day. From there they moved on to their main objective at the German-held village of Mametz. Fighting alongside their colleagues of the 91st Brigade, they helped overcome the German defenders, but not without sustaining heavy casualties. Out of the 796 men of the battalion who had begun the day, by the end of it 472 of them had become casualties. A total of 709 of the regiment's men died on the first day of the Battle of Somme. Having first arrived in France in November 1915, they remained there until being sent to Italy in November 1917, where they were at the war's end.

Private 251120 Harold Dunbar, who was 22 years of age, and serving with the 1st/6th Battalion, Manchester Regiment, died on 15 September 1917, and was buried at the Étaples Military Cemetery. I would imagine many of his comrades from the 22nd Battalion would have no doubt attended his funeral. During the month of September 1917, the Manchester Regiment as a whole lost a total of 237 of their men. This including forty-one who died as a result of fighting in France, and 183 who died in Belgium. September was an extremely difficult month for the Manchesters.

Private 51723 John Matthew of 21st Battalion, Manchester Regiment, who was 29 years of age, died on 12 October 1917 and was buried at the Étaples Military Cemetery. His wife, Edith, who lived at 39 Oswald Street, Rochdale, received a letter from No. 18 General Hospital, situated at the Étaples camp in France. The letter said: 'Private Matthew passed away very quietly leaving no messages. He will be buried with full military honours in the British Military Cemetery at Étaples.'

Private Matthew had enlisted in the army in April 1917 and arrived in France in August 1917. One of his brothers had been killed while serving in France in 1916, while another was also serving in the army at the time of Private Matthew's death. It is interesting to consider how the Manchester's would have reacted towards the soldiers at Étaples, who they had been sent to bring back in to order. Would they have obeyed the orders of their officers, or taken the side of their fellow soldiers who had become embroiled in the mutiny? Either way, it is thankfully something we will never know the answer to.

Private 20817 Peter Smith, Military Medal, of the 22nd Battalion Manchester Regiment, was 34 years of age, having enlisted in the army on 30 November 1914, in Manchester. He first arrived in France on 15 November 1915, and went on to become one of the battalion's wounded from the first day of the Battle of the Somme, the following year. After having had his wounds treated, he was sent to the 30th Infantry Base Depot at the Étaples camp. He found himself back at the camp the following year when he was taken ill, and admitted to No. 26 General Hospital.

Peter Smith served with the 22nd Battalion throughout the entire war, amassing a total of four years 109 days service before being demobbed on 18 March 1919. During his wartime service he saw action numerous times on both the Western Front and in Italy. He was a married man who had six children, two of whom were born during the war, meaning that he was home for a spell on leave in September 1916 and again in January 1918.

The 1st Battalion Welsh Fusiliers served on the Western Front for the entire war, and besides being a hard-fighting and well-respected group of men, they were also well known for the number of writers and poets to have served in the regiment. This included Siegfried Sassoon, who was one of the most famous poets of the First World War. He was also an extremely brave soldier who on 27 July 1916 was awarded the Military Cross, the citation of which read as follows:

> For conspicuous gallantry during a raid on the enemy's trenches. He remained for one and a half hours under rifle and bomb fire collecting and bringing in wounded. Owing to his courage and determination all the killed and wounded were brought in.

Sassoon was also later recommended for the Victoria Cross, but it was an award he never received.

Chapter Four

Étaples Through the Eyes of the Press

The first real mention of Étaples in the British press wasn't in relation to the military camp, but I still believe it is worth noting as it talks about Étaples as a quaint little French seaside town at a time when, although the war had begun, it had not quite become a reality for many people.

The article was on page 4 of the *Birmingham Daily Gazette* dated Saturday 8 August 1914:

War Scenes in a French Village
By an English Lady

> Safe on English soil! It is almost a miracle that we have got here, and the nightmare of it all still shadows my eyes, while the misery and fear and anxiety for others is utterly uncontrollable, for though I escaped from France with my husband and little child, all relatives and friends who were with us have been left behind bottled up without stores of food at Paris-Plage, at Trepied, at Cueq, and the other villages around Étaples.
>
> Away in quiet villages, taking daily tram trips to the seaside and occupying ourselves with the paddling of children in the sea, we did not awaken early enough to grave personal danger, though somewhat saddened by the distress of the

> poor French peasants and others who were telling of how their sons had been called to be ready in case of war.
>
> It was, to me, merely a sign of French thrift and foresight should prices go up when on Friday I saw two women, nearing sixty years of age, at a small villa that had been built for the family, themselves shovelling in to their cellar tons of coal; for they were women who I knew had thousands of pounds at their back. Four sons had gone with their neighbours, and there were no men to do the work.
>
> Still in a colony of English friends we lingered happily enjoying our holiday from London till the bomb of 'general mobilisation' fell.
>
> Playing with children on the sands at Paris-Plage on Saturday afternoon the air was suddenly electrified, a black cloud blotted out the sun, and the stillness that comes before a storm made itself felt. A woman agonised and distraught, looking like a ghost, dashed over the stretch of sand to me. 'Madame, you are French? War is declared.' And at that moment the solemn tolling of a bell in the town at the back verified her fears. I rushed after her to try and calm her, then I saw from the sea and the immediate wide stretch of sand, the whole populace of hundreds of bathers, and those sitting about their tents and cabins, sweep up in to the town, dumb with anxiety. The drummer had posted up in the town all the mobilisation notices written in ink, for there was no time for printing.

Appreciating that the war had begun while this lady and her family had been on holiday in France, it had been common knowledge that a war with Germany was on the horizon, and it was and had been for a long period of time, a case of 'when?' and not 'if' there was going to be a war. With that in mind it is incredible that other than maybe on the south coast of England, they had plans to go away on holiday at all, especially somewhere on the French side of the English Channel. Surely in such circumstances the idea would be to distance yourself as far away from a warzone as was possible, and not to head directly towards it, especially when that meant having to escape would require a boat to get you back home to safety. Maybe the lady and her family liked to live dangerously, or didn't read the newspapers that much, or were simply too apathetic to comprehend the real threat that a war actually posed to them.

> Holiday makers, trades-people, mechanics in their shops, road menders by the way, servants in hotels, all read the notice and turned solemnly away, not back to their work but to their homes; for many had to leave at six o'clock on Sunday morning, and they had to take with them their horses and different trappings, their automobiles, all that would be of use to their country. Not a sound, not a word from anyone, even children were mute.

The speed at which Étaples suddenly became one of the most important locations in France was as impressive as it was unexpected.

> Étaples was the nearest railway station and we made our way there as quickly as possible. At the station there were thousands of people, and of luggage literally a thousand trunks and boxes. All who could clamber in to one train going to Paris might depart that night, and for those who had return tickets there might be one train going from Paris to Boulogne in the morning. The ticket office was absolutely closed, and at mid-day on Sunday the station would be closed.
>
> Our only hope was to stay near the railway station.

Her story continued with a description of conveyances of all types having been commandeered by, or on behalf of, the French government, and a sombre night with the front doors of homes and businesses nearly all open, with people sitting around as if in shock. All the local men aged between 18 and 48 were readying themselves for mobilisation and war, as the women sat around not speaking, as if they were mute, wondering when and if they would ever see their loved ones again, some instinctively knowing that it would be the last time they would set eyes upon them.

The next morning the woman, her husband and daughter, not only managed to acquire some tickets, and as if by magic, a short while later an empty train rolled in to the station. Without a word between them they made a dash for the train, barging their way past the stationmaster in the process. Running across the tracks they managed to clamber into one of the carriages while the train was still moving, such was their urgency to get on board.

Even at such a time, 'an official' was in hot pursuit demanding money to let them remain on the train. A discussion in broken French took place along with some hand gestures and facial expressions, before coin changed hands, and all was once again well in the world, at least for a train official at Étaples railway station. But his victory would no doubt be a short lived one.

The craziness of the moment continued as the train left the station with just three members of an English family on board, uncertain of their destination while hoping it would be Boulogne. There was concern for sure, when every few yards they saw a French soldier, distinctive in their sky-blue uniforms, patrolling along either side of the train, fingers crossed that the train would keep moving and get them to Boulogne without any further surprises.

Having reached Boulogne they were fortunate enough to find a British registered vessel that was on its way back to England. They discovered by talking to some of their fellow passengers that some of them had spent two days waiting on a train platform in Paris, repeatedly trying to catch a train to Boulogne without any food or water, but it had been impossible with each of the trains being packed to the rafters.

Many of these poor unfortunate souls only had the clothes that they stood in, either unable to pack before they left, or having discarded their baggage to make room in the train's carriages for other people like them, trying to make good their escape from France and the fear of a quickly advancing German Army.

The unnamed vessel was only designed to carry 700 passengers, but there were well over 1,000 on board by the time they left for Folkestone, and the quayside was already chock-a-block with others waiting for their turn to board the same vessel when it returned from England.

The husband, wife and child had made it safely back home, but only by the 'skin of their teeth', and were in no rush to once again return to Étaples. By the end of the war, there were many British, Australian, New Zealand and Canadian troops, thinking exactly the same thing. Soon after this family made good their escape, the area suddenly lost its appeal as a holiday destination and quickly became more about wounded British and Commonwealth soldiers who had arrived at Étaples railway station from areas of the Western Front on their way to the base hospitals in and around Boulogne.

An article in the *Nottingham Journal* newspaper, dated Monday 28 December 1914, concerned a Miss Margery Boot who was in the process of setting up a kitchen and café at Étaples for the wounded British soldiers.

> Today Miss Margery Boot leaves Nottingham on her errand of mercy to organise the Kitchen and Café at Étaples, and to find the necessary funding for the establishment and upkeep of which readers and friends have so generously contributed. The idea of the café, as we have before described it, is to provide needed little attentions in the way of comforts, warm food, and nourishment and suitable drinks like cocoa, chocolate, tea, coffee, milk, etc., for the wounded soldiers from the western battlefield who come through Étaples station daily on their way to the base hospitals in and near Boulogne.

Miss Boot will be assisted in her Samaritan work by a number of young ladies who are enthusiastic and well qualified, and the scheme has the warm approval of the French military authorities, and the English Red Cross Association. It is highly gratifying that the Fund should already have reached a sum sufficient to justify the work being taken in hand at once, and readers will be glad to hear of the work and success of the Café in the near future. Naturally a considerable amount more is needed to reach the sum necessary to place the undertaking on a satisfactory basis, but our friends may, we are sure, be depended upon. It will be cheering knowledge for all the donors to the fund this Christmas time to know that they have helped to this end so quickly. More shillings will be gratefully acknowledged; and gifts of provisions will be exceedingly welcome.

The provisions principally required are cocoa, sugar condensed milk, compressed soups, meat extracts, cigarettes and matches. Gifts of cigarettes will be especially welcome. It must be remembered that practically all the provisions will have to come from England, as only bread and butter, and very small supplies of these, are just now obtainable in the district around Boulogne. Any amount from one shilling upwards will be thankfully received. Not a penny of the money subscribed will go towards the personal maintenance of the party.

Subscriptions may be addressed to
Miss Margery Boot
St Heliers
The Park
Nottingham
or to the Express Office, Parliament Street, Nottingham.

On Saturday 6 October 1917 the *Dumfries and Galloway Standard* newspaper included an article about a local man who had been wounded in action while serving in France.

> Mrs Halbert, 1 Nicholson Place, Annan, has received a letter from her husband, Private William Halbert, Hampshires, stating that he has been admitted to 18th General Hospital, Étaples, suffering from shrapnel wounds in the face received in action in France on 27th September. He states that his right eye has suffered, and that he has received 'a peppering'. This is the second time he has been wounded, and he has been in France for two years. Before the war he was engaged with Mr Mitchell, Baker, Annan.

Private 16981 William Halbert, first arrived in France on 27 July 1915, as a member of the 1st Battalion, Hampshire Regiment, having enlisted on 2 September 1914 at Dumfries.

His army service record shows that his punishment for two acts of indiscipline was seven days field punishment No. 2, for being out of his billet, improperly dressed and providing a false name to a member of the Military Police. It also shows that he spent twenty-nine days in hospital, between 6 July 1916 and 4 August 1916, after receiving gunshot wounds to both his hands. He also spent a further period of time in hospital between 30 March and 3 May 1918, having been wounded in action for a third time.

The *Dumfries and Galloway Standard* newspaper dated Saturday 6 October 1917, also carried an article about an Amos Goodman.

> Gunner Amos Goodman, RFA, son of Mrs Goodman, 51 Copland Street, Dalbeattie, was admitted on 27th August to the Canadian General Hospital, Étaples, suffering from severe shell wounds on head and mouth. This is the second occasion on which Gunner Goodman has been wounded. A brother is serving with the Gordon Highlanders, and another is with the ASC.

A check of the Commonwealth War Graves Commission website, shows a 22-year-old Gunner 73005 Amos Goodman serving with the 21st Battery, 2nd Brigade, Royal Field Artillery, died on 29 April 1918, the son of William and Agnes Goodman of 9 Grainger Street, Darlington. He is buried at the Lijssenthoek Military Cemetery, which is situated in the West-Vlaanderen region of Belgium. On the balance of probabilities, I would say it is the same man.

On Saturday 20 October 1917 an article appeared in the *Londonderry Sentinel*, in relation to a public meeting which had taken place the previous day at Londonderry's Guildhall in connection with the mayor's appeal for funds.

The meeting was open to one and all, members of the public as well as local dignitaries, for which there had been a large attendance. Its purpose was to help raise funds on behalf of the British Red Cross Society and St John of Jerusalem Ambulance Service.

Much was discussed, from the sums of money which had been raised in previous years, to the sacrifices which families and communities continued to make in giving up their young men to go off and fight in the war, and to the subsequent hardships that those same young men had to endure, while doing their bit to help achieve an Allied victory.

In 1917 the Red Cross needed £60,000 per week, or £6 per minute, to be able to carry on all of the work they had undertaken for the nation's wounded servicemen, and it wasn't the government who financed the work.

Mr McCorkell, the County Director for Donegal advised the meeting about work undertaken by the Red Cross at the Étaples camp. At that time, the camp's Red Cross-funded 'Londonderry Ward' was able to cater for 584 beds, eighty-eight of which were for officers, and the remaining 496 for men from the 'other ranks'. The hospital sometimes had to take in many more cases than they were set up to treat at any one time, so plans had been made that if such an eventuality occurred, the number of available beds could be increased to 750.

Throughout 1916–17, the number of medical cases treated there was 8,503, and the surgical cases during the same timeframe were 6,380.

It was interesting to note that during the same time that Étaples had a less than positive reputation for its treatment of abled-bodied men, regardless of whether they were on their way to the Western Front or on their way home, the treatment provided by its medical staff to the sick and wounded that filled the wards of the camp's many hospitals, was second to none.

It must have been nice for the ordinary people of the city of Londonderry to know the good they were doing for the wounded soldiers who were being treated on the Londonderry Ward at Étaples, as a direct result of the monies they were providing for the Red Cross.

Mr McCorkell finished his speech by saying that he hoped that the people of the City of Londonderry continued with their charitable donations, with the same level of giving as they had in previous years, so that the Red Cross could continue their important work on the Londonderry Ward at the Étaples camp.

On the evening of 19 and 20 May 1918, a German air raid took place on the Étaples camp, which resulted in more than 300 casualties. On Tuesday 28 May 1918, Mr Bonar Law, the then leader of the Conservative Party, informed the House of Commons that a report on the matter had been asked for, but had not yet been received. The Commonwealth War Graves commission website shows that 211 members of the Australian, British, Canadian and New Zealand armed forces, died over the course of those two days.

The *Whitby Gazette*, dated Friday 23 August 1918 carried an article about an inquiry which had been made in parliament the previous week.

> A correspondent of the Morning Post writes with reference to an inquiry made in the House last week by Commander Wedgewood in connection with the Étaples outrage, 'evidently with the intention of palliating the German crime,' that a niece of his was a nursing sister in the Étaples hospital at the time of the attack. She states that the German aeroplanes first dropped their bombs with disastrous effect on some of the huts filled with wounded, and when the nurses and orderlies got out as many patients as they could

> from the wreckage and laid them in the open, the enemy aeroplanes kept circling over the camp so low that the nurses could actually hear the commands given by the German officers! After they stopped dropping bombs they started with their machine guns, firing on the men on the ground, and a number of nurses were shot.

The *Irish Independent* dated Saturday, 8 January 2000, included an article concerning the 1918 global flu epidemic.

> An investigation in to the 1918 global influenza epidemic, which killed an estimated forty million people, has shown it started in an army camp in France in the middle of the First World War.
>
> A team of medical scientists has painstakingly trawled through historical records and discovered, among previously secret files, that there was a mysterious respiratory infection at a military base in Étaples, in north-west France, in the winter of 1915–16.
>
> The findings suggest that a lethal pandemic of flu, which doctors are expecting to occur again, may take several years to 'smoulder' in a densely populated area before bursting into a global conflagration.
>
> The 1918–19 influenza outbreak, the most lethal epidemic of infectious disease in modern times, has traditionally been called Spanish flu or the Spanish lady, because it was in Spain that doctors first identified it as a new form of the respiratory illness.
>
> However, scientists have since acknowledged that the name is probably a misnomer, because the epidemic's origins

were just as likely to be elsewhere in the world. It is not known, for instance, that the epidemic occurred apparently simultaneously in places as far apart as South Africa, India, and Indonesia.

Up to one billion people were believed to have been infected, and otherwise healthy young adults were among the many millions who died in what has become one of the greatest mysteries in medical science: what made that strain of virus so lethal and where did it come from?

Trying to find the answers has led to the frozen bodies of some of the known victims being exhumed from permafrost burial grounds in Spitzbergen in Norway and Alaska to isolate the 1918 virus.

John Oxford, Professor of virology at St Bartholomew's and the Royal London School of Medicine, and his colleagues believe that the Étaples camp became the birthplace of an influenza strain two years before its devastating spread, as infected soldiers were dispersed.

As if enough people hadn't been killed as a result of the fighting of the First World War, millions more died by nothing more devastating than a virus.

The *Dundee Evening Telegraph* dated Friday 14 February 1930, contained a rather interesting account of the Étaples mutiny.

Story of Étaples Mutiny
Scottish Sergeant shot by 'Red Cap'.
Mistake that led to Riots

An account of the alleged mutiny at Étaples in 1917, in which Scottish soldiers were said to have figured so prominently, is given by S.J.C.K. in the Manchester Guardian. The story is perhaps the fullest that has yet been published, and many may recall the writer's reported succession of remarkable incidents.

One striking point is the alleged shooting of a Highland Sergeant in mistake by a Red Cap, who had fired at a New Zealander fleeing from arrest.

Late on an afternoon in September 1917, a New Zealander was strolling over the railway bridge towards Étaples with his arm round the waist of a WAAC. His behaviour irritated a military policeman stationed on the bridge to examine the leave passes of soldiers wishing to visit the town.

An altercation arose as the result of which the New Zealander, having offended the red-capped authority, was arrested and marched off to prison just outside the camp.

The dispute had been followed from the start by the usual group of soldiers hanging about on the outskirts of the camp. These men considering that the loathed Red Cap was ill-treating a Tommy, soon gathered in a crowd near the hut, jeering at the policeman and urging the prisoner to escape.

The Shot

As the uproar increased the New Zealander encouraged by the shouts of the crowd, made a dash for liberty and dived in to a group of Highlanders.

The policeman, pestered and excited, raised his revolver, fired at the fugitive, missed him, and killed a Jock sergeant! That's when the trouble began. It happened that the sergeant was a popular and much respected veteran, the very opposite (as the view believed) of the military police, who apparently remained in safety at the base camp and bullied the fighting soldier on his way back to the trenches.

The killing of a fighting soldier suddenly brought to a head all the long accumulated hatred for the Red Caps. As the news reached the infantry base depot of the Scottish regiments, the Jocks poured out vowing vengeance, and the Red Caps disappeared from the railway bridge.

Riotous Crowd

Then an order came that all junior officers were to turn out and clear Étaples of rioters. We found the riotous crowd in a street near the bridge trying to break in to a café where some military police were believed to be sheltering.

A plucky Scottish Colonel forced his way to the doorway and spoke to the men, promising that the guilty policeman should be punished and urging the men to return to their depots without annoying civilians.

A day or two later, the article states, the bridge over the railway was unguarded, and Étaples was open to those who ignored the order that all leave was stopped, and a number of men had left the camp and gathered in the town. When this crowd of rioters, for they really were rioters now, had pushed unhindered through Étaples they reached the main road bridge in impetuous mood, and swept along towards the square.

Walked through

A Major ordered his men in to two ranks, with their front rank kneeling, with rifles loaded and bayonets at the ready, after they had walked out to remonstrate with the mob.

The ringleaders passed on, arguing with him and pushing him back, till his men had to put up their bayonets to avoid wounding him. The rioters pushed aside the rifles, went through the guard, and continued towards Le Touquet.

Meanwhile a smaller mob came to the railway bridge over the river. The young officer in charge ordered the mutineers to go back or be fired upon. Some hesitated but the ringleader took no notice of the instruction and approached the youngster with a threat about the river being handy for drowning such puppies.

Given the KO

As he came close, up went the officer's fist and the man was laid out. While he was being bound, his comrades retreated hastily, giving no more trouble, though hatred of the Bull Ring and of Police authorities was fairly general; in fact, an officer was put under arrest in a club for beginning to make a speech of sympathy with the so called mutineers.

The whole protest was against the alternately dull and harassing life of the huge, unwieldy camp at Étaples rather than against the war itself; against those believed to be shirkers at the base rather than against service in the line.

An interesting article, which describes the events during the Étaples mutiny in vivid detail, but sadly, for some reason it does not provide the name of the individual who was responsible for its writing.

On Thursday, 25 August 1955, a really interesting story appeared in the *Dalkeith Advertiser*, that was born out of a visit made by a local County Councillor, Mr Stuart Blackie Syme, to New Zealand and Australia to meet up with old army friends and colleagues, some of whom had emigrated from Dalkeith and the neighbouring villages to Australasia after the First World War.

Mr Syme, who enlisted in the army on 5 January 1911, when he was just 29 years of age, had been a sergeant (278881, 695, 7658) serving with the 7th Battalion, Princess Louise's Argyll and Sutherland Highlanders. He was wounded in action on 8 May 1916. This eventually resulted in him being discharged from the army on 6 April 1918, as his wounds meant he was no longer physically fit for wartime military service.

After being discharged from hospital in Boulogne, Mr Syme was detailed to escort two New Zealand prisoners, Gunner Julian and Driver Power, to the Divisional Base Camp at Étaples. On handing the two men over to the Military Police, he was given a written receipt by the sergeant of the guard, Ernest Thoval Stout, which he had in turn kept as a souvenir, along with other items, as part of his wartime military service.

While in Invercargill in New Zealand he met a Scotsman by the name of Jimmy Orr, who during the war had been a company sergeant major in the Black Watch. Having emigrated to New Zealand, Orr had become an accountant, working for a firm that had been founded by a man named Stout – which turned out to be the same man who had handed Mr Syme the receipt back at Étaples.

Stout had begun the war as a private in the New Zealand Infantry, and had been wounded in action while serving at Gallipoli. He had arrived in France in April 1916 from Alexandria, and soon found himself at Étaples where he spent a couple of weeks before moving on to Armentieres. It was during his stay at Étaples that he found himself in the position of sergeant of the guard.

Stout finished the war with the rank of captain, having being wounded for a second time while serving in Flanders. His other claim to fame was that his uncle, Sir Robert Stout, had been a previous Premier of New Zealand.

Mr Syme posted the receipt to Mr Stout, which he happily kept. So it was that a piece of paper which began its journey at Étaples in France, made its way to Scotland, and ended up in New Zealand – back with the man who had written it at Étaples.

The man who went on to became famous and known as 'Mr Ballroom Dancing', Victor Silvester, had his life story, which included his military service during the First World War, serialised in the *Liverpool Echo.* During his career, which lasted from the 1930s through to the 1980s, his records sold a staggering 75 million copies.

Silvester was born on 25 February 1900 at Wembley in Middlesex, the second son of a vicar; he enlisted in the British Army in September 1916, when he was still only 16 years of age, although he informed the recruiting officer that he was 20. He became a private in the Argyll and Sutherland Highlanders and was sent out to France where he saw active service at the Battle of Arras, which took place between 9 April and 16 May 1917. During his time at the front he sadly had to endure the experience of being a member of a firing squad on more than one occasion, shooting fellow soldiers who had been convicted of being deserters, some of whom were not much older than himself.

His real age was eventually discovered while he was still serving in France, which resulted in him being immediately sent back to England. En route from the front he spent two weeks at Étaples; luckily for him, he had absolutely no idea of the camp's fearful reputation. Silvester continued his story in the *Liverpool Echo* on Thursday 13 November 1958.

> I was sent back to the big military base at Étaples, where my duties consisted of peeling potatoes, cleaning out latrines and Waiting at night in the camp's officers' mess.
>
> The mess sergeant began by instructing me in the technique of giving change to officers who paid for their drinks in cash. I was shown how to arrange the coppers in a symmetrical pile, at the same time spreading the silver all over the tray. The reason was that once an officer had had a few drinks

> his attention would be caught by the copper and he would miss some of the silver on the tray, which was also of silver.
>
> However, I did not profit by this practice. Our orders were to take the trays straight back to the bar, where the tips and left change would be put into a box, a hawk eyed corporal watching to see that no soldier waiter slipped anything into his own pocket. I believe it was shared by the sergeant and a couple of warrant officers in charge.'

Just that little piece about Étaples and Sylvester's experience while briefly being there, show that the camp wasn't just a horrendous place to be. His time there was somewhere around the August of 1917, meaning it was during the relevant time period when Étaples was in the build-up to the mutiny of September 1917.

Sylvester's case was interesting insofar as when it was discovered that he was only 17 years of age, he should have been sent home and dismissed from the army, because he had clearly lied about his age on enlisting. Instead, he was sent to the camp at Étaples while the military authorities decided what to do with him.

For a soldier to serve in the British Army during the First World War, they had to be 18 years of age at the time of their enlistment. Underage boys managed to creep in under the radar for two basic reasons. First, the British Army needed as many fighting men as they could possibly get, and second, recruitment sergeants were paid a sum of money for every man they signed up. It is believed that there were somewhere in the region of 250,000 'boys' who managed to enlist in the army, despite clearly not being the required 18 years of age. The youngest being Sidney Lewis who was reputed only 12 years of age. He went on to see action during the Battle of the Somme, which began on 1 July 1916.

Somewhat surprisingly, Sylvester was not discharged from the army for having lied about his age and sent home, instead he left the comparative safety of Étaples and was sent to Italy to serve in the First British Ambulance Unit. While serving as a stretcher bearer in fighting at

Sella di Dol, Sylvester was assisting to evacuate wounded Italian soldiers during a bombardment of their positions by Austrian and German artillery units, when he himself was wounded by a shell blast. Despite his own injuries, he continued attending to the wounded Italian soldiers until they were all safely removed from danger. So impressed were the Italian authorities with Sylvester's act of bravery that they awarded him the Italian Bronze Medal of Military Valour. The announcement of the award was made by the Italian Minister of War on 30 November 1917, which meant that he was still too young to be serving at the front, as his 18th birthday wasn't until the following February.

Chapter Five

Air Raids on Étaples Camp

An air raid took place over the Étaples area between 2230 hours on 19 May 1918 and 0100 hours on 20 May 1918. The raid resulted in some parts of the camp being struck. Two bombs landed in the part of the camp where elements of the 1st Battalion (1st Life Guards), Guards Machine Gun Regiment, were staying. This resulted in forty-six members of the Guards being killed with a further eighty-three wounded. All of those killed were buried at Étaples Military Cemetery.

Trooper 4493 Ainsle, James, 26 years of age.
Corporal of Horse 2673 Boylin, G., 29 years of age.
Trooper 4596 Fenwick, Roger Mansel William, 20 years of age.
Corporal 3647 Finley, William Reginald, 25 years of age.
Lance Corporal 3004 Finnimore, Herbert Henry, 24 years of age.
Corporal of Horse 2798 Fleming, J.H.
Trooper 3917 Geeson, Harry, 27 years of age.
Trooper 4556 Hamilton, A.
Corporal 4556 Goddard, D.
Trumpeter 2556 Godwin, C.F.R.
Trooper 3548 Gray, John, 25 years of age.
Trooper 4258 Green, Lionel, 20 years of age.
Trooper 4224 Hammond, Norman William, 23 years of age.
Trooper 3640 Clay, E.
Trooper 3370 De Renzy, T., 24 years of age.
Trooper 4439 Downing, A.F.
Trooper 3396 Douglas, R., 24 years of age.

Trooper 3032 Taylor, Henry, 22 years of age.
Trooper 4150 Toberty, H., 32 years of age.
Corporal of Horse 2960 Waspe, W.E., 25 years of age.
Trooper 3681 Turner, H., 20 years of age.
Squadron Quartermaster Corporal 2027 Vessey, G.N., 43 years of age.
Trooper 3082 Vye, George Samuel, 28 years of age.
Squadron Corporal-Major 2052 Webb, W.S.
Trooper 4422 West, Richard Hemming, just 19 years of age.
Trooper 3779 Worne, Leonard William, 21 years of age.
Trooper 3029 Young, Alexander Edward, 23 years of age.
Trooper 3371 Hobday, W., 34 years of age.
Trooper 4025 Honey, Joseph Henry, 22 years of age.
Trooper 2883 Hopper, Thomas, 23 years of age.
Squadron Quartermaster Corporal 2315 Horsman, Albert, 35 years of age.
Trooper 3947 Isherwood, Frederick John, just 19 years of age.
Trooper 3860 Keeble, Henry David, 22 years of age.
Trooper 3725 King, Cecil Percival, 23 years of age.
Trooper 3503 Lawrence, Bret, 27 years of age.
Trooper 3430 Ray, Francis Harry, 23 years of age.
Corporal 3995 Riddler, Wilfred Harry, 20 years of age.
Trooper 4161 Robb, Angus, 22 years of age.
Trooper 3149 Rowland, Albert Joseph, 23 years of age.
Trooper 3609 Royce, Eric Hooper, 22 years of age.
Trooper 4280 Simkins, Frederick John, 20 years of age.
Trooper 4169 Spendlove, Henry Lenton, 23 years of age.
Trooper 3812 Staniforth, Herbert Edward, 27 years of age.
Trooper 3089 Mariner, Ernest, 24 years of age.
Trooper 3014 Moody, George Samuel, 22 years of age.
Trooper 3278 Ogbourne, Harry, 20 years of age.

This incident just went to show how Étaples camp and death, sadly, almost went hand in hand with each other. If it wasn't down to the mutiny, unrest, and military hospitals that resulted in a soldier losing his life, then it was down to air raids such as the one of 19/20 May 1918.

A month later on 31 June 1918, a question was asked in the House of Commons in relation to the air raid of 19/20 May, by Colonel Josiah Wedgwood, the Liberal Member of Parliament for Newcastle-under-Lyme, who had also been on active service in France and Belgium during 1914, as well as the Dardanelles, where he was awarded the Distinguished Service Order for his actions during the landings at Cape Helles on 25 April 1915.

Colonel Wedgwood asked the Under Secretary of State for War whether he was aware that the German government had justified their bombing of the Étaples Hospital on the night of 19/20 May by the allegation that there had been no 'Red Cross' shown on any of the tents or buildings that made up the hospital complex.

The Under Secretary of State for War, and the Liberal Member of Parliament for Ross and Cromarty, Mr Ian Macpherson, replied that he was aware that the German government had so justified the bombing of Étaples Hospital. He added that he had also seen photographs published in a German newspaper with the intention of proving that there was no visible Red Cross sign on the Étaples hospital on 21 May, but this had been rectified by 27 May. Mr Macpherson further stated that German photographs of such a nature were rarely conclusive, and that in any case the hospitals at Étaples were again bombed on the night of 31 May/1 June 1918 in spite of Red Cross signs, which German evidence showed had been in existence on 27 May.

Colonel Wedgewood pushed the Under Secretary of State for War on the matter, and asked him if he was personally satisfied that the Red Cross sign was in place at Étaples on 19 May, Mr Macpherson replied that he was. There was a further air raid on 31 May 1918, when there was further loss of life.

But it has to be said that this was by no means an isolated incident, as Étaples camp was the target of many a German air raid, especially towards the latter months of 1917 and into the early part of 1918. It isn't clear what the main purpose of the raids was. It could have been to attack the railway lines that serviced the camp, or it could have been a direct attempt to kill those British military personnel who were in the camp at any one time, as the Germans would have been well aware of the large numbers of British and Commonwealth troops that it catered for. But despite the death and destruction these air raids caused, ultimately the attacks on the camp were of little strategic purpose. Maybe their main achievement was that of the negative effect on morale that they had. After the improvements in conditions and attitude that had been made to life in the camp in the immediate aftermath of the mutiny and troubles of August and September 1917, Étaples experienced a period of relative calm, but the air raids, or more the threat of them, was sufficient to ensure that the men's nerves were never totally as they should be. The threat of air raids only properly began to diminish as the war entered its final months, by which time the camp and the surrounding areas had been given the added support of anti-aircraft units and buildings were reinforced with sandbags.

As an aside, two men who served with the Labour Corps and who were killed as a result of German air raids while serving at Étaples, had something in common.

Private 447677 Robert Paterson of the 842nd Company, Labour Corps, died at the camp during an air raid on 21 May 1918, having previously served as Private 290992 of the 7th Battalion, Black Watch (Royal Highlanders). The other soldier was, Private 442019 Alexander Thomas Paterson of the 939th Company, Labour Corps, who had previously served with the 1st Battalion, Black Watch (Royal Highlanders), who died of his wounds on 1 June 1918. The pair were not related.

Étaples as a military base was, the German's would argue, a legitimate target for their aircraft to attack, which to a degree was understandable, but it was when they failed to distinguish between a legitimate military target and medical facilities which not only brought shame on Germany, but caused anger and outrage among British, Canadian, New Zealand and Australian authorities, because to them it simply was not a tactic of war that should ever be used.

Etaples Camp May, 1918.

Right: A cartoon of the Bullring.

Below: Men preparing to play cricket.

Above: Major Douglas Reynolds, VC. Buried at Etaples Military Cemetery.

Left: Lieutenant Eric Fitzwater Williams, who was threatened by Private Jesse Robert Short during the Etaples mutiny.

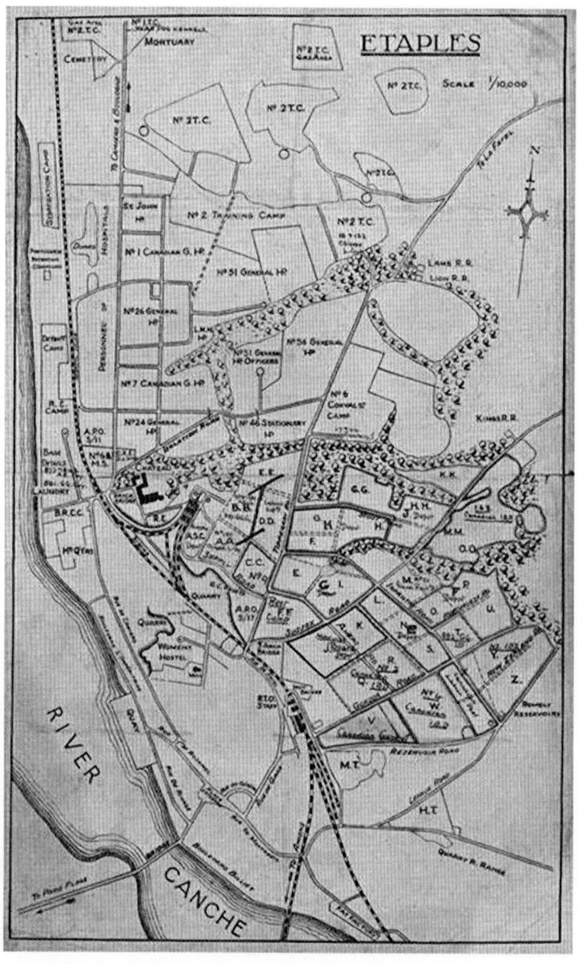

Map of Etaples Camp.

Etaples Military Cemetery, located within the main Camp.

Above left: Percy Toplis: was or wasn't he at Etaples Camp?

Above middle: Unknown soldier of the Royal Welch Fusiliers outside a hut at Etaples camp.

Above right: Unknown soldier of the Royal Welch Fusiliers in a posed studio photograph.

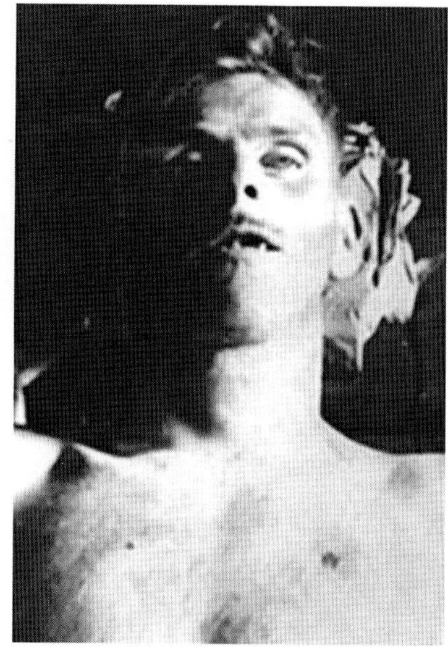

Above left: Soldiers carrying the coffin of nursing Sister Margaret Lowe to her grave at the Etaples Military Cemetery, May 1918.

Above right: Mortuary photograph of Percy Toplis.

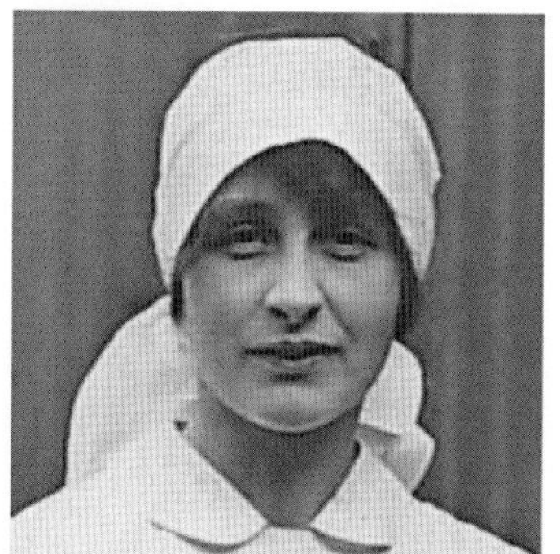

Above: Soldiers practicing with a Vickers machine gun at the Bullring, Etaples camp.

Left: VAD Nurse Vera Brittain, who worked at Etaples camp between August 1917 and April 1918.

Above left: Etaples camp with both tents and huts.

Above right: Soldier training with his dog in the sand dunes on the part of Etaples Camp that backed onto the beach.

King George V visiting Etaples Military Cemetery, 14 May 1922.

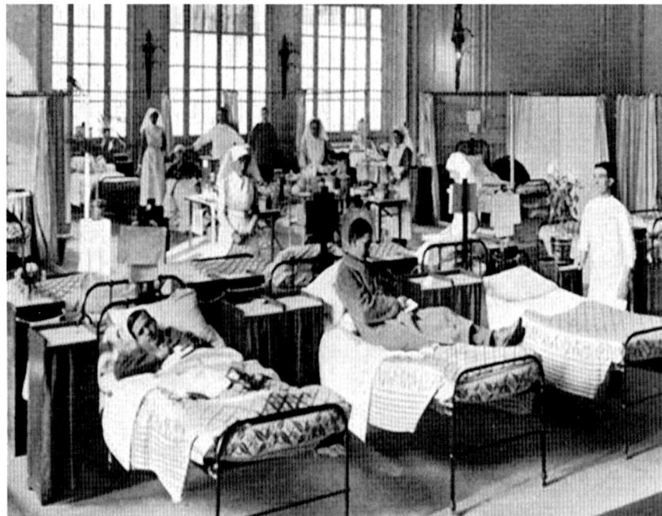

A ward at the Etaples Military Hospital.

Etaples Camp 1916.

Above: Etaples Camp dog section.

Below left: Member of Royal Military Police, having a shave 1915.

Below right: Graves being tended to in the cemetery.

Memorial service in 1918.

Above left: Nurses preparing to play cricket against the men.

Above right: Memorial service in 1918.

Right: Men preparing for physical training.

Running for the ambulances.

Sports day, wood chopping competition at New Zealand Base, Etaples 1918.

Left: Sports day 3 August 1918. Nurses involved in a game of tug of war.

Below: Training at the Bullring in the snow.

Chapter Six

Étaples Enquiry

In relation to the Étaples mutiny, a good example of the difference between how those at the bottom end of the military chain and those at the top thought, came in the form of Douglas Haig. On the last day of the mutiny, 14 September 1917, referring to his lunch he wrote in his diary, 'drank several glasses of wine, port and brandy'.

True leaders ask nothing of the men they lead, that they would not be prepared, willing and able to do themselves. There are no records that I am aware of which show sergeants and men from the other ranks being able to take time out for a nice long, drawn-out lunch, where they were able to sit back, chill out while smoking a Cuban cigar and drinking copious amounts of alcohol, without a care in the world.

If news of the troubles at Étaples had leaked out, it could have led to similar behaviour among British soldiers elsewhere. In the circumstances it is really quite shocking that Haig himself did not attend the camp and speak to the men personally. That way he could have addressed their concerns, given them some assurances, and seen first-hand the conditions these men had to endure, and how they were being treated by elements of the staff who worked there.

The fact that Haig didn't do this, regardless of how busy he was with other important war matters, suggests to me that he didn't take this course of action because he wasn't really that bothered by it. Haig was a disciplinarian not a pacifist. By way of example, one only has to look at the large number of death sentences that he approved and signed, which sent over 300 of his own men to their deaths. It is correct to say that for many of those men, they had a far from fair trial. Some had no legal representation or anybody to speak for them. Some did not even fully understand what was going on, or the seriousness of the situation they were in, of which Haig would have been well aware. But still he let these men die.

Personally, I don't believe Haig was really that concerned about the welfare of his men at Étaples, or anywhere else for that matter, because to him, men were there to be used for his own egotistical ideas. If one man, ten men, or even one hundred men were killed, all he really thought about was where their replacements were coming from and how quickly they could get to where they were needed.

At breakfast on 2 July 1916, Haig was informed by one of his staff of the number of casualties which the Allies had sustained on the first day of the Battle of the Somme. When told that there had been some 50,000 Allied casualties, of whom 20,000 had been killed, there were no tears of sorrow, shock at the number killed, or even the thumping of his desk. Instead, he commented on how such figures were in keeping with the strength of the enemy they were up against, and the width of the front across which they were fighting. Without one flicker of emotion, he simply carried on with his breakfast.

There was not even the consideration of changing his tactics, or thoughts about how the number of casualties might be reduced for the following days and weeks of the battle. As far as he was concerned, he had actioned his plan of attack and the casualties would be what they would be. The men under his command simply became numbers, and those who were killed or wounded were simply part of the casualties his staff officers had estimated there would be.

His thinking wasn't much different at Étaples. To him, how his men were treated by the camp's instructors and members of the Military Police was of no real concern. There was a chain of command and men, as far as he was concerned, did as they were ordered by their superior officers and that was the end of the matter. There was no debate, it was simply a case of 'do as you are told'.

The Battle of the Somme is a good example of how outdated Haig's tactics were. The week before the start of the fighting, Haig had ordered an artillery bombardment of German defensive positions to soften them up in readiness for the infantry attack. There were two problems with this. First, a percentage of the artillery shells that were fired never exploded, they simply landed with a thud and made a small hole in the ground; second, the Germans simply dug themselves deeper underground to protect them from the falling bombs. Another aspect of this is that it would not have taken a genius to work out what would happen as soon as the artillery bombardment finished. The Germans certainly did. They immediately brought out their machine guns and waited for the Allied attack which they knew was coming.

Although Haig did not go to Étaples to intervene in the mutiny, he was obviously kept up to date with the events which unfolded there. Although never admitting so in public, Haig was sufficiently concerned about the situation at Étaples, to make immediate changes there, so as not to alienate British soldiers who would find themselves at the camp in future months and years.

The infamous 'bull ring' was closed down. The man in charge of the camp, General Thompson was quickly replaced, and in October 1917, soldiers on the Western Front were given a 1*s* per day pay rise. In 1915, infantrymen were earning 1*s* 6*d* per day, and a member of the Machine Gun Corps were earning 2*s* 9*d* per day in 1916. It has to be pointed out that at the same time, Members of Parliament earned £400 a year (£159,000 in today's money), even more if they were a member of the War Cabinet. This was a staggering sum of money when taking in to account they are currently paid about half of that today.

After 1914, five million industrial workers enlisted in the British Armed Forces. They brought with them the class antagonism they had been schooled in by the four years of the Great Unrest, immediately beforehand.

In the summer of 1917, the British and their allies established a metropolis of war extending from the coast of Belgium to the headwaters of the River Somme. Some two million men, women, soldiers, and labourers were gathered in a vast array of tents, huts, hospitals and prisons.

Brutality

It was an Army drawn from the four corners of the British Empire, and a microcosm of its brutality. In training grounds known as 'bullrings' new recruits received as little as nine days instruction before being thrust to the front.

Étaples in north east France was the core of this metropolis. The troops were subjected to a fierce regime by officers of the blood and bayonet school.

War poet Wilfred Owen described it as a 'kind of paddock where beasts are kept a few days before the shambles'.

Soldiers old, new and injured were marched and double marched across the dunes. Their main meal was two slices of tinned beef, two biscuits and an onion. Denied the pleasures of Étaples town (known by the troops as 'eat apples') one soldier described the experience as 'like passing through hell'.

Military police who had rarely been to the front meted out discipline and 'there was always someone tied to a gun wheel'.

A good example of the feeling of discord between senior British Army officers and the rank and file was a quote by Field Martial Douglas Haig: 'Every position must be held to the last man. There must be no retirement. With our backs to the wall, and believing in the justice of our cause, each one of us must fight to the end.' I do not believe that quote was intended to be taken literally by senior British Army officers, including Haig himself, as they were nowhere near the front lines when fighting was actually taking place. Haig also stated: 'As a matter fact we have to take special precautions during a battle to post Police to prevent more unwounded men than are necessary from accompanying a wounded man back from the firing line.' Haig did not clarify if the same precautions applied if it was an officer who was being carried from the battlefield.

As previously mentioned, it now transpires that all documentation in relation to what is known as the 'Haig Inquiry' into the events at Étaples during September 1917 have been lost. Personally, I do not think this makes too much difference from a historical point of view. I cannot believe there would have been anything too startling in the official findings; they would have endorsed the actions of the Military Police on duty at the camp at the time of the mutiny. In relation to the treatment by the instructors and the Military Police of those who transited through the camp, it would have been seen as in keeping with British military discipline. The blame for the mutiny would have been placed squarely on the shoulders of those soldiers who decided to disobey the orders of their officers.

Even though changes were made in the regime at Étaples and the 'bull ring' swiftly done away with, there is no way that the authorities would have publicly admitted any wrongdoing, or accept responsibility for what went on there. Any written report that would have come out of the Haig Inquiry would have no doubt been biased and one sided towards the British Army, and would have brought nothing new to the 'discussion', other than frustration and contempt from the families of those men involved in the events of more than one hundred years ago.

Chapter Seven

Vera Mary Brittain

Vera Brittain was a nurse during the First World War serving with the Voluntary Aid Detachment (VAD), and was one of those working at Étaples at the time of the mutiny in September 1917.

She began working as a part-time volunteer nurse with the VAD on 18 September 1915, serving with the London 268 Camberwell Section. Her wartime service with the VAD saw her working in Malta, France and England. Her first posting was at Camberwell Military Hospital, where she worked from 18 September 1915 to some time in September 1916, after which time she volunteered for overseas postings. She didn't have to wait long and before the end of the month she had already been shipped out to work at a military hospital in Malta, to attend to those soldiers who had predominantly been wounded, or who had fallen ill, while serving during the Gallipoli campaign. She remained in Malta until June 1917, before being sent out to France, where she arrived on 3 August 1917 and worked at the Étaples camp and was there at the time of the mutiny, and all the way through until 20 April 1918. It was while working at Étaples that Vera was awarded her Scarlet Efficiency Stripe. This was for VAD nurses who were under contract to the War Office, to denote that they had been certified as 'efficient' by their matron and Commanding Officer.

She then appears to have taken a well-deserved five-month break from nursing, as she returned to England. On 25 September 1918 she began working at the 5th London General Hospital, which had opened in March 1915, starting, in essence, as 200 beds at St Thomas' Hospital in Lambeth Palace Road, London. Vera worked there for just over a month, leaving on 28 October and moving immediately to the Queen Alexandra's Military Hospital, Millbank, where she remained until 28 March 1919.

Most of the men admitted to the 5th London required detailed surgery and as the war progressed, so did the need for more and more hospital beds. To accommodate this, huts were erected in the hospital grounds and used as additional wards. This meant that 568 men and ninety-four officers could be treated at any one time. Before the 5th London finally closed its doors on 31 March 1919, it had treated 11,396 patients.

She wrote about her wartime experiences in her memoir, *Testament of Youth*, which covered the period 1900–25, and was published in 1933. She wrote about how female personnel, which in the main were nursing staff, 'were shut up in our hospitals to meditate on the effect of three years of war upon the splendid morale of our noble troops.' She also wrote in reference to the mutiny that 'numerous drunken and dilapidated warriors from the village battle were sent to spare beds, for slight repairs'. According to Vera, the mutiny at Étaples did not actually end until the middle of October 1917. It was her opinion, based on what she had witnessed at first hand, that 'the mutiny was due to repressive conditions and was provoked by the military police.'

The memoir is her own personal wartime story, but having lost her brother, a good friend of hers, as well as her fiancé during the war, it is also about her baring her soul. It comes across as part of a healing process for her, especially with the added memory of her time spent at Étaples.

Vera's brother, Edward Brittain, Military Cross, was killed in action on 15 June 1918, when he was just 22 years of age. At the outbreak of the war he had enlisted in the British Army and was commissioned as a 2nd Lieutenant in the Sherwood Foresters (Nottinghamshire and Derbyshire Regiment). He was sent out to France in early 1916, and was wounded on 1 July 1916, the first day of the Battle of the Somme, when he was shot in the left shoulder and right thigh. His injuries were such that it was necessary to send him back to the UK for further treatment at the 1st London General Hospital, where Vera was working at the time.

His award of the Military Cross was due to his actions on that day, and the citation for his award, which appeared in the *London Gazette* dated 20 October 1916, stated that it was given for 'conspicuous gallantry and leadership during an attack, during which he was wounded, but continued to lead his men with great bravery and coolness until a second wound disabled him.'

He remained in England recovering from his wounds and recuperating, before returning to France and the Western Front on 30 June 1917, where he was once again straight back into the thick of the action. In August 1917, he was sent out to serve on the Italian Front. He was shot dead on 15 June 1918, during the Battle of Piave River.

Vera's fiancé, Roland Aubrey Leighton, became a Second Lieutenant in the 4th Battalion, Norfolk Regiment, on 21 October 1914, when he was just 20 years of age.

Vera and Roland had first met in 1913; the relationship developed and they were formally engaged in August 1915. He was promoted to the rank of lieutenant and transferred to the Worcestershire Regiment on 26 March 1915, and was involved in fighting around Ypres in Belgium. In December 1915, Roland was inspecting the wire in front of a trench at Hebuterne in the Pas de Calais region of France, when he was shot by a German sniper. The bullet didn't kill him, but he was left severely wounded by the shot, which struck him in the stomach and also damaged his spine. He underwent surgery at nearby Louvencourt, but only survived a matter of hours before dying of his wounds later that day, 23 December 1915.

Chapter Eight

Percy Toplis

Francis Percy Toplis, more commonly known by his middle name of Percy, was born on 25 September 1896, in Chesterfield, Derbyshire, to Herbert and Rejoice Toplis who, being poor, could not afford to bring him up, so he was raised by his grandparents.

His school years appear to have been a mirror image of what he went on to become. At school he was noted for being somewhat of a bully, and was often caned for his conduct and behaviour. At 13 years of age, Toplis left school and despite his unruliness, managed to acquire himself a blacksmith's apprenticeship at a colliery in the mining village of Blackwell in Derbyshire, but once again his ill-discipline and bad attitude cost him his position.

What is known of Toplis is that in 1915 he enlisted in the Royal Army Medical Corps, with whom he served as a stretcher bearer on the Western Front, with his first 'action' coming at Loos in Belgium. I don't believe this was during the Battle of Loos, which took place between 25 September and 8 October 1915, because the 11th Division, which included the 33rd, 34th and 35th Field Ambulance units of the Royal Army Medical Corps, moved to Gallipoli in July 1915, although which unit Toplis was attached to is unclear. This was, however, a journey that Toplis most definitely took, the only point that isn't clear, is exactly when.

An article on Wikipedia mentions that he deserted soon after August 1918, when he was in Blackpool, yet I have seen a police report dated 18 October 1918, which shows that he had deserted while in Salonica on 15 June 1918, and that he was wanted for purchasing a gold watch with a 'dud' cheque. His army service record has not survived, which would have included the units he served with, and when and where he served, providing an exact timeline of where he was at any given time throughout the war.

Over the years Toplis's name has become synonymous with the story of the Étaples mutiny, but the question about him that really needs answering is: was he the 'Monocled Mutineer', and was he ever actually at Étaples? The only time there has been any mention of a monocle and Toplis, is when the clothes on his body were being searched after he had been shot dead.

The Monocled Mutineer was published in 1978, which was about the part Toplis was purported to have played in the Étaples mutiny. It caused much debate as to whether it was a non-fictional account of the events, or a fictional one. The doubt as to which it was appears to have arisen out of claims that Percy Toplis wasn't even at Étaples at the time of the mutiny, but actually on his way to India.

In researching and writing about Toplis, I have not found any definitive information or proof that he was ever actually at, or anywhere near Étaples at the time of the mutiny in September 1917. That being said, the obvious question has to be: how was Toplis connected with the mutiny at Étaples? The following article appeared in the *Police Gazette* on Friday 18 October 1918.

> 8. Nottingham (County). – For obtaining at Hucknall, 27th ult., a gold bracelet watch by worthless cheque on London County and Westminster Bank, Beckenham Branch, which he signed as 'John Williams'.
>
> No. 47551 Pte Percy Toplis, aliases Captain or Lieutenant Jones. Topley, Williams, Taylor, etc., a deserter from RAMC., Salonica, since 15th June 1918, age 23, ht. 5ft 7 or 8in., h. sandy, clean shaven but may have small tuft of hair under nostrils, one tooth missing front upper jaw; dress, uniform of 1st Lieut., new Sam Browne belt, soft cap with ASC badge, leather lined, British Warm coat, brown high topped boots and spurs, wearing three blue and one red chevron and

> enamelled Mons ribbon. Since desertion has posed as an officer and has stayed at Matlock, Folkestone, Southampton and in London. Photograph can be seen on application.
>
> Warrant issued.
>
> Information to the Chief Constable, Nottingham.

On Friday 1 November 1918, this brief article also appeared in the *Police Gazette*.

> 9. Nottingham (County). – PERCY TOPLIS, Case No. 8, 18th ult., is identical with FRANCIS EDMUNDSON, CRO No. S 139484, age 22, ht. 5ft 6in., c. fresh, h. sandy, e. blue. A collier; native of Chesterfield. Pre-con of fraud, larceny, and attempted rape at MANSFIELD, CHESTERFIELD, ALFORD (Percy Toplis) ANNAN (Francis Edmundson). And PATELY BRIDGE (William Denison).
>
> Warrant Issued.
>
> Information to Supt. Harrop, Nottingham.

This appears to be the one and same Percy Toplis, and would have no doubt been in the build-up to when he was finally located and shot by the police.

Some time at the end of 1918, Toplis was sentenced to a term of imprisonment for fraud at Nottingham Assizes. On his release from prison he rejoined the army in early 1920 when he enlisted in the Royal Army Service Corps and was stationed at Bulford Camp, which is situated on Salisbury Plain in Wiltshire. He worked at the camp in some kind of admin capacity. It was while he was there that he had the opportunity to continue his criminality, and he certainly didn't hold back. As a clerk he found himself at the centre of a 'pandora's box' of items that he could utilise, or rather steal, for his own benefit. It wasn't long until he used, or rather abused, his position to start making money for himself by selling fuel, specifically allocated for military purposes, on the black market. Even though it was 1920, fuel was still heavily rationed. It was clear by his actions that he had absolutely no empathy for any of his colleagues, as one of the other 'criminal enterprises' he embarked as a way of making money, was to falsify military documents, appertaining to soldiers wages, which allowed him to steal the salaries of some of the colleagues with whom he served at Bulford camp.

Toplis must have been a very calm and calculated individual. He had acquired a colonel's uniform which he took to wearing when he went to 'visit' women in either the village of Bulford, or the nearby town of Amesbury. The fact that he might be spotted in his colonel's uniform by others from his camp, of whatever rank, was of no concern to him whatsoever.

Toplis was certainly no fool, and he realised that it would only be a matter of time before his nefarious activities were discovered. With this in mind he went 'absent without leave' on the evening of 24 April 1920, sometime after 9 pm. This was also the same evening and time frame during which taxi driver Sidney George Spicer was shot dead at Thruxton Down. He was last seen at 9 pm driving off to pick up a fare at Amesbury, who wanted taking to Andover. When Spicer's body was later found discarded in a hedge like rubbish, it was discovered that he had been shot through the back of the head.

A connection between what was obviously the murder of Sidney George Spicer and the desertion of Toplis from the nearby Bulford Army Camp was quickly made when a number of statements were taken from soldiers stationed at the camp. One of which mentioned Toplis talking about acquiring a car by foul means or fair, and another, which was extremely damning for him, from a soldier who went on a joyride with Toplis in what turned out to be Spicer's vehicle, although the other man had no idea this was the case.

The inquest in to Sidney Spicer's death found that he was wilfully murdered and that Percy Toplis was the man who had committed the murder. This was an extremely unusual finding to come out of an inquest, and it is believed to be the first time that an inquest has declared a man guilty of a murder, in his absence and without him ever having being interviewed or allowed to respond to such a serious allegation against.

This was at a time when a conviction for murder would have seen the individual concerned, dangling at the end of the hangman's rope.

Toplis was also a suspect in a number of other unsolved murders around that time, but was shot dead by the police on 6 June 1920, without having ever being interviewed about any of those crimes.

The *Aberdeen Press and Journal*, dated Wednesday, 9 June 1920, carried a large article about Percy Toplis.

How Percy Toplis Made His Last Stand
Graphic Story of Revolver Duel
Identity With Tomintoul Miscreant Fully Established

It was definitely established by the inquest held at Penrith yesterday that the man who was shot dead there by the Police, the man who wounded a Policeman and a farmer at Tomintoul, and Percy Toplis were one and the same.

It is also suggested that it was Toplis who murdered Nurse Shore in the London-Hastings express, last January.

The full story of the last act in the drama was told at the inquest, at which the jury returned a verdict that Toplis was justifiably killed by the Police, while fleeing from justice.

Last Scenes
Pathetic Moments Before The Inquest

After completing a full investigation of the circumstances of the Tomintoul-Penrith-Toplis mystery, I am able to disclose information casting new light on what Inspector Gorman, one of the ablest officers in the Criminal Investigation

Department of Scotland Yard, described to me today as the most remarkable contribution made since the opening of the century to the crime records of the country.

Beyond a shadow of a doubt the man who murdered the taxi-cab driver in the country lane at Andover, the miscreant who wounded Constable Greig and Mr Grant, the farmer, in the deserted moorland cottage at Tomintoul, and the youth who met his death in a revolver duel with the Police at Plumpton, a Hamlet five miles from here, are the same person, Percy Toplis, who deserted from the mechanical transport section of the Royal Army Service Corps at Bulford Camp.

This morning people from Banffshire, who saw the Tomintoul assailant, and relatives of Toplis brought from Derbyshire were taken in to the cabin of the weights and measures yard beneath the Town Hall of Penrith to view the body. In accordance with the procedure followed at inquest preliminaries, they were cautioned not to disclose their decision till called in to the witness-box later in the day.

When a sister of Toplis left the mortuary she was in a pathetic state of anguish, and weeping unrestrainedly. By the courtesy of the Police I was permitted to see the dead man. The face had none of the features which ones mind would associate with the countenance of a murderer. It was that of a sunny-tempered boy, smiling as if in a happy dream. But the corpse was that of Toplis, or a counterfeit made by nature to imitate, in minute details, the physiological peculiarities of the cunning and callous criminal.

There was the mole under the left side of the chin, the growth which earned for Toplis the nickname among his chums of 'The Barrack-broom,' and on the back of the right hand a

> scar mentioned in the circulated description of Toplis. It was only the length of a vesta match, but it answered correctly. Across the knuckles was a newer wound, a tear caused by a strand of barbed wire. Above all there was the clue of the teeth. Toplis had two incisors missing. In the mouth was a small, recently and imperfectly made plate with two artificial dentures corresponding to the two that Toplis had missing.

This article was certainly in keeping with the day, in that it was extremely lengthy and detailed, and took up a quarter of the page, in what would be described as a 'broad sheet' newspaper which was eight pages in total, and included only two photographs and eight small drawings. There was definitely a need for such articles, to ensure that there was sufficient 'copy' to fill the number of pages in the newspaper.

> On the floor stood a grimy canvas kitbag found in a wood outside the town last night and containing a khaki uniform.
>
> At the Police station I was shown a trayful of articles found on the body and produced at the inquest. Of first importance was a memorandum book of such size as to be more appropriate to a lady's vanity bag. Courtesy to the Coroner's Court demanded that the more intimate pencilled entries on its pages cannot yet be told, but it is sufficient to say that the contents show Toplis served on the Western Front during the War, and he was at Bulford on the night of the terrible tragedy in that locality. In one of the pockets a Sunday newspaper was found, folded at a column containing an account of the Banffshire shooting tragedy.
>
> There was also a motor driver's licence issued at Bulford in the name of Thomson. Toplis had only a half crown in money in his possession, and hung from a cord round his neck was a locket containing a single photograph of a

> smiling beautiful young woman. An inscription on the back read – 'Remember perfect times. Yours all, Maudie.'

It is clear from reading through this article that the unnamed reporter from the *Aberdeen Press and Journal* had an extremely helpful contact within the police, to be provided with such detailed and personal information about Toplis, down to being allowed to examine his dead body.

Constable's Story
Leeds Officer who belongs to Kildrummy

> Prior to the opening of the inquest, the Police intimated that Constable James Watson, Leeds City Police, had identified the body as that of the man who made his escape from the Tomintoul district. Constable Watson was proceeding from his father's farm, Milton of Kildrummy, to Alford by the Strathdon motor bus on his way to Leeds after his holidays last Wednesday, when Toplis joined as a passenger. According to his statement the Constable was completely convinced the man was the same.
>
> Dr Macdonald, the medical officer who examined the body after the shooting, is it may be noted, a native of Banffshire.

Toplis was shot dead by the police on the afternoon of Sunday, 6 June 1920, and the inquest in to his death took place on Tuesday, 8 June 1920 in Penrith, when colleagues of his from the Bulford Camp, positively identified him.

The Inquest
Police story of Revolver Duel

> All doubts as to the identification of the man who was shot by the Penrith Police on Sunday afternoon at Plumpton, was set at rest today at the inquest, when witnesses from Bulford Camp,

definitely declared him to be Francis Percy Toplis, aged 23, the Private in the Army Service Corps for whom a hue and cry has been raised throughout the country in connection with the murder of the motor driver Spicer, near Andover, on 26th April last. The body was also identified as that of the man who attempted to murder a Policeman and a farmer in Banffshire on Tuesday last.

The story told by the Police witnesses at the inquiry, which was held at the Penrith Town Hall, was one of the most dramatic heard by a coroner's jury, and was listened to with tense interest by a crowded court.

In the end the jury returned a verdict that the deceased was justifiably killed by a revolver bullet at Plumpton by Police officers on 7 June 1920, who were attempting to effect his arrest while a fugitive from justice.

Witnesses from the North of Scotland who identified the body as that of the man concerned with the Tomintoul shooting, were John Mackenzie, gamekeeper, who was shot at by Toplis; Peter MacIntosh, blacksmith, Tomintoul, who repaired the fugitive's bicycle and lent him 5s; and Christopher Rodd, merchant, Tomintoul, to whom Toplis, when in hiding, came for provisions; and Alexander Thom, cycle Agent, Glenkindie, with whom the dead man left his bicycle on the trip down to Strathdon, in exchange for £1.

Details concerning the man were first given by Mrs Winifred Bowler, of Shoreham, who said he was her brother. He was a blacksmith by trade, but of late had been in the Army.

Sergeant Harry Smith of the ASC, stationed at Bulford, spoke to the deceased having been in his company. He was he said a deserter.

Superintendent James Cox of Hampshire Constabulary, detailed the circumstances of the murder of Spicer at Thruxton, and told the court how Toplis made his way in to South Wales with a companion, and how afterwards Toplis paid his companion's fare back to Bulford and left Swansea himself on the Paddington train. The description of the body of the man in the mortuary, he declared, tallied with that of the man wanted for the murder.

The discovery of Toplis in the Penrith district was graphically described by constable Alfred Fulton, of the Westmorland Constabulary, stationed at Low Hesket, eleven miles from Penrith. He said he was on duty on the highway near that village on Sunday afternoon when he saw a soldier sitting down near a dyke. He walked towards him, and the soldier got up and moved on towards Penrith, throwing his pack over his shoulder. The witness questioned him and the man replied that he was going to Penrith, producing a duty ticket from Aberdeen, and explaining that he was on escort duty.

He noticed that the description of Toplis and the man he had spoken to were the same, and jumping on his bicycle, he rode after him, but missed him. Two young ladies told him that a soldier had just passed them, and Fulton discovered him in a plantation, and said to him, 'Hullo, boy, is this as far as you have got?'

The man jumped up, and pulling a revolver from his pocket, shouted out, 'Hands up!' Fulton was bound to obey, and the deceased said to him, 'It is me you are looking for, is it? If you are, I am Toplis. It was me who shot the Policeman and farmer, and if you act the same you go too.'

> He compelled Fulton to drop his handcuffs and truncheon on the ground, and then said Fulton, 'I decided that he was not going to shoot me as he lowered the revolver.'
>
> Fulton told him to get out of the district, and he replied, 'I will kill or be killed.' Eventually the deceased left him. As he did so Fulton noticed that the deceased was changing in to civilian clothes.

Constable Fulton appears to have been a very calm character, although at the time Toplis was pointing the revolver at him, especially as he had just admitted having shot two other men, it is anyone's guess as to how he was feeling in the pit of his stomach. There would, I suggest, have been a period of time when he was looking straight down the barrel of the revolver Toplis was pointing at him, when he thought that he was about to die, the fact that he didn't panic or break down, shows what a remarkable character Fulton must have been.

> The story was taken up by Superintendent Oldcorn, who said that the last witness reported the incident at once to him, and he ordered him, with Inspector Ritchie and Sergeant Bertram, to drive in a motor car to the place spoken of by Fulton. He first handed them revolvers, warning them to use them with discretion. He explained that he thought it necessary to arm them, as Toplis was known to be a desperate man. This action had been approved by the Chief Constable.
>
> Inspector William Ritchie recited how, when they were driving towards Castlestars, past Plumpton, they passed the deceased, who was in plain clothes. After passing him they returned and repassed him, and when doing so the deceased placed his hand to his hip pocket. Witness told the driver to

push on and after going some way the three of then got out of the car and hid behind a building.

I looked round the corner and saw the deceased coming, and when he got opposite me, I sprang right at him, making no exclamation until I got well on the road. I said, 'Stop, Pull up!' He apparently noticed me at the same time, and he sprang forward and commenced running. Still running, he turned round and at a range of about five yards, fired twice direct at the Police officer. He was turning round to fire a third time when Bertram and I fired, and Toplis fell, being so close that he fell into my arms.

When searched, witness added, 'there were found upon him a monocle, a pawn ticket for a watch, and two motor licences, as well as a ticket from Aberdeen to Wendover.

This statement was corroborated by Sergeant Bertram, and also by Charles Norman de Courcy Parry, late of the Seaforth Highlanders, and son of the Chief Constable, who obtained permission to accompany the Police party on their search.

Mr Parry said that he was riding a motor cycle, and carried an automatic pistol in his pocket. He saw Inspector Ritchie jump out at the man, with Sergeant Bertram just behind him. Deceased ran about three yards, and, turning about, shot at Ritchie, the bullet passing over Ritchie's head.

Deceased continued running, and again fired point blank at the Inspector, who was gaining on him. Witness heard two shots then, and two or three from the Police, and deceased dropped in to Ritchie's arms.

Parry's involvement in the search for Toplis was somewhat unusual by today's standards, especially when it transpired that not only was he armed, but with a Belgium automatic pistol that he had brought back from active service during the war, when Ritchie and Bertram were only armed with revolvers, quite possibly ex-military officers' Mk V .455 Webley pistols, left over from the war. For me, this leaves an unanswered, and now an unanswerable, question, 'why was Parry there at all?' The Police had sufficient men, and could have quite easily, and reasonably quickly, amassed more manpower to go after Toplis, but the chief constable's son went instead. It just doesn't make sense.

> Witness expressed the opinion that had the Police not fired, Ritchie would have been killed, as he was so close to him.
>
> Dr Eddington stated that deceased was shot through the heart, and Deputy Chief Constable Barron, produced a remarkable diary found on the deceased.
>
> The diary detailed Toplis's movements from the beginning of the year, and mentioned visits to Bristol, Cardiff, Swansea, London, Swansea (robbery), Bristol again (monocle bought for 15s at Bath) Chepstow, Salisbury, Southampton, Winchester, Bath, Freshford (with Dorothy at Bulford on April 24), and so on down to May 24, when there was written in the diary, 'Hunting West Wales, some hopes'.
>
> Witness produced a bullet which fitted the deceased's Webley revolver, which he (witness) found 125 yards from the scene of the affray, and also said he had found a kit bag in the bracken which contained the uniform the deceased was wearing when Fulton first saw him.
>
> Replying to a question, he said that if the Police had wanted to shoot Toplis they could have done so before Toplis saw

> them. Inspector John Goodall, one of the Banffshire Police, identified the body as that of the man who shot the constable and the farmer in Banffshire.

It was certainly a good decision for Ritchie and Bertram to be armed when they went looking for Toplis, as it is quite clear from reading through those accounts that if they had approached him without the support of their revolvers, both men would no doubt have either been seriously injured or killed by him, knowing that if he was taken alive, he would definitely face the 'gallows' for the murders he had already committed.

For Toplis, being shot dead in a shoot-out with the Police was always likely to be the way it was going to end for him. The longer he was at large, the bigger the risk was to the police and members of the public who he came across.

> In the course of his summing up, the Coroner said there could be no doubt that the body the jury saw was that of Toplis. The jury must come to the conclusion that there was necessity for the action taken by the Police. The case came exactly within the scope of justifiable homicide.
>
> The jury returned a verdict as stated, and added that they considered the Police acted with discretion and care, and that their conduct was worthy of praise. They congratulated the officers on their intelligence and promptitude.
>
> The funeral of Toplis takes place tomorrow. Mr Grant may travel to Penrith today for the purpose of identifying the body of Toplis, as that of the man who shot him.
>
> The inquest in to the death of Toplis took place on 8 June 1920, and he was buried the very next day in an unmarked grave near the top of the Beacon Edge Cemetery in Penrith.

Passion for Crime
Murderer's Career of Crime

Percy Toplis was a Zolaesque type of criminal, a man in whom the passion for crime was deeply ingrained and to whose ends even murder formed no obstacle.

As George Smith, who drowned his brides in a bath, was the most heartless character in recent criminal history, so Percy Toplis was the most daring and callous. Like Smith and other notorious criminals, Toplis was very vain.

People have likened him to Claude Duval, Dick Turpin and Jack Sheppard. He showed many points of resemblance.

He was only 21, and he had lived a life of crime since he left his mother's apron strings. When he was only 12, he obtained money by false pretences at Mansfield (Notts), and for this he received six strokes of the birch-rod. Four months afterwards he was in Chesterfield, where he stole 36 newspapers. He was bound over.

At 15 he went to Dumfries, where he was sentenced to 10 days imprisonment for stealing two railway tickets. He then gave his name as Francis Edmundson. Six days after coming out of prison, this 15-year-old criminal went to Pateley Bridge, Yorkshire, where he was caught stealing a purse containing money. He then gave his name as William Denison, and was sentenced to a months imprisonment.

In the following year he attempted to rape a girl at Lincoln, and for this he was sentenced to two years hard labour.

Toplis was a 'wrongun' from the very beginning. Many of his early crimes brought him little or no financial gain. He committed many of those crimes for no other reason than that he could. He was an opportunist, he does not appear to have given much, if any, thought to what he was actually doing or why. It was more a case of something appearing in front of him and the desire to take it just because he could, was a very powerful and all-consuming aspect of his criminality. On the assumption that he was identified and caught for the crimes, he was not a very good criminal either.

During my thirty years as a police officer, there were many occasions where my colleagues and I dealt with individuals referred to by 'intelligence reports' as being a 'prolific' shoplifter, burglar, thief, etc. The reality was they were only classed as being prolific because of the number of times they had been arrested, which actually meant they were not very good criminals at all. Many of these individuals put absolutely no thought in to what they were doing, if they had, the chances are they would never have been caught. This led me to draw another conclusion.

During my time as a policeman, there were a number of individuals I dealt with who had been given the perennial tag of 'prolific', but the reality was, they couldn't cope on the 'outside', where, in essence, they were a nobody. In prison, they were told when to get up, when to eat, and when to go to bed. They had no bills to pay and all their meals were provided, and they associated with like-minded individuals, some of whom would look up to them, with some kind of hero worship status. I believe Toplis came in to this category.

> Less than two years ago, in October 1918, he was arrested at a London railway station and sentenced at Nottingham, to six months imprisonment for obtaining a gold watch by giving a worthless cheque.
>
> These are crimes he was convicted for. How many others he was responsible for, it is impossible to say. But it is known that at various times he took the names of Jones, Topley,

> Williams, Denison, Taylor and Edmundson. Only a few months ago he joined the Royal Army Service Corps as a Private, and after many criminal adventures, including the thefts of motor cars, he deserted.
>
> Then on April 24 he shot Sidney George Spicer, the motor car driver, on the road near Andover (Hants), drove the motor car to Swansea, and then roamed about the country a fugitive from justice. He kept a loaded revolver in his pocket to sell his life dearly.
>
> Scotland Yard have evidence, says the 'Daily Chronicle,' to suggest that Toplis was the murderer of Miss Shore in the London-Hastings express on January 13 last.

What doesn't make any sense about Toplis is what happened in his life that changed him from being a petty criminal, whose main criminality was to steal and defraud, to being a cold-blooded killer, who took life without an apparent care in the world.

One of Toplis's brothers, Leonard Toplis, who was ten years older than Percy, was serving with the 10th Battalion, Notts and Derby (Sherwood Foresters) Regiment, when he was killed in action on 6 August 1916, on the Western Front.

There were 'rumours' in relation to Toplis that his death had somehow come about as the result of a 'vendetta by the political establishment', which had seen him set up for Sidney Spicer's murder because of his involvement in the Étaples mutiny. I do not believe there is any substance to this allegation, first, because there is no direct evidence that proves beyond all reasonable doubt that he was ever at Étaples at any time. If he was at Étaples, and involved in the mutiny, then why wasn't he arrested and put before a court martial. It also has to be remembered that within a matter of days of the mutiny coming to an end, nearly all of those men who had been at the camp and were able-bodied, found themselves on the Western Front involved in such fights as the Battle of Passchendaele and the Battle of Cambrai, which collectively saw British casualties in the hundreds of thousands.

The publication of Allison and Fairley's *The Monocled Mutineer* in 1978 gave rise to a lot of renewed interest in Percy Toplis. In 1980 the British playwright Howard Barker wrote and produced a play, *Crimes in Hot Countries* which featured Toplis; in 1986, the BBC screened a four-part adaptation by Alan Bleasdale of Allison and Fairley's book. Other books about Toplis followed, the most recent, *Who Shot Percy* by Jim Cox OBE, was published in 2018.

Chapter Nine

Edwin Woodhall

Who was Edwin Woodhall, and what part did he play in the story of the Étaples mutiny of September 1917? Woodhall was a Special Branch detective based in Boulogne, having joined the counter espionage team of the Intelligence section in 1915. The part he plays in the Étaples mutiny is a very significant one because despite there being no officially documented paperwork proving beyond all reasonable doubt that Toplis was ever at Étaples, Woodhall mentions having arrested him in his 1929 book, *Detective and Secret Service.*

In the immediate aftermath of the Étaples mutiny, Woodhall was transferred to the Military Foot Police, and along with a number of his colleagues, tasked with rounding up those who had been involved in the mutiny. Woodhall refers to these mutineers as 'delinquents' and 'absentees'. He explains how he discovered Toplis in a café and then set about taking him back to the camp's detention centre to carry out further enquiries and to ascertain the man's true identity, only to discover the following day he had managed to escape by tunnelling his way out under the fence through the soft and pliable sand that the camp stood on.

It would appear that Woodhall did not know the identity of the man who he had detained at the time, other than he was a man who he suspected of either been involved in the camp's mutiny, or who was possibly a deserter. This point leads me to ask the obvious question – did Woodhall actually detain Toplis at all, or did he simply include this claim to make his book more interesting and saleable? Without the inclusion of the story about Toplis, it is questionable as to whether any publisher would have found it either an evocative enough subject, or a financially marketable enough topic to publish.

The problem I have with Woodhall's claim is that it just doesn't add up. The main reason for this is the lack of any record or documentation, that I know of, which confirms Toplis was at Étaples before, during, or after, September 1917. Another reason is because he is known to have deserted in Salonica, Greece, on 15 June 1918, where there were a number of Royal Army Medical Corps hospitals. If he was supposedly at Étaples in September 1917 as a deserter, but wasn't seen after he supposedly 'escaped' from custody having been detained by Woodhall, how is it that nine months later he is then back with his 'unit' in Salonica. I am not aware of any report stating that Toplis was recaptured after his 'escape' from Étaples, but that's possibly because he was never captured in Étaples in the first place.

I believe that in Toplis, Woodhall had simply seen an opportunity to make some money by writing his book. He would have known that most, if not everything, he wrote about would be impossible to corroborate, so if that was the case, what did he have to lose by writing it? Absolutely nothing at all. The question is when did he came up with the idea for the book? He had credibility because he was at Étaples at the time of the mutiny, although it was not officially classed as such at the time. This might have been because to those in authority at the camp, the events of September 1917 were nothing out of the ordinary. The only real difference on this occasion was one of the Military Foot Police shot dead a British soldier, accidentally or otherwise.

Chapter Ten

Hansard

On 5 February 1918, Lord Ribblesdale raised a discussion in the House of Lords on the topic of a canteen that had been established and run by Lady Angela Forbes and some of her friends at the Étaples camp. In essence, Lord Ribblesdale was singing the praises of the canteen and all it stood for, against a backdrop of slander and rumours that had then been subsequently spread about Lady Forbes's good character. Here is just a small part of what Lord Ribblesdale had to say.

> Let us go to Étaples, not to that modern creation, that wonderful example of the industry and the power of our military machine, but to the old Étaples that some of us know, the dirty squalid town by the sea. She lived near there, and when she was going home one day she saw that the potential values of Étaples as a camp and training ground were being discovered. There were a few base details there, and also the workmen from Holloways, who were building the huts. She saw them hanging about, and spoke to them. They told her that they had nowhere to go except the lowest possible public houses in Étaples. Again, she was prompt to recognise human needs. That very day she took the biggest house in Étaples and started an institution there which was crowded by day. The workmen had nowhere to get breakfast. She and her children cooked breakfasts for the workmen every morning at five o'clock.

Some of what Lord Ribblesdale had to say was particularly interesting, and very relevant to the troubles of September 1917:

> Then came the time when her hut was built. To show your Lordships how very little importance she attaches to her work at that hut, I will tell you one thing. I notice that Lord Rhondda is not present; but in January, 1917, when she saw there was a food shortage approaching, she went to her head officer and said, 'In my opinion these canteens are a mistake in view of the shortage of food. They ought to be turned into recreation rooms, and I am ready as the person running the most successful canteen, to offer mine as a first sacrifice if the other institutions will follow in my footsteps.' But there were other more powerful institutions. Perhaps the late commissioner for food economy will tell you about them. Anyhow, her idea was not carried in to effect. There was a great camping ground at Étaples where 10,000 men were drilled every day. They came long distances. There was no food for them, and it was considered right that they should have rations. The difficulty was how, in half an hour, to feed 10,000 men. Being supposed to be somewhat of an authority on catering, they asked her advice. She suggested that, though they could not feed them altogether in one place, they might quite easily feed them in parties of 1,000 in ten different places. Feeling that she could not devote the profits that she made out of the men in the evening better than to their welfare in the morning, she offered to build fourteen huts where these men could be fed and entertained. Her offer was accepted, and she organised and started the scheme, and I believe that the whole system was admirable for discipline.

What was staggering about reading that piece was the camp had been developed by officials who knew full well the large number of men who would be going through it at any one time, and yet one of the most, if not the most, important aspects of camp life was meal times, which did not appear to have been catered for. If it hadn't been for the intervention of Lady Forbes and her colleagues, the troubles which took place at Étaples in September 1917 may well have taken place much sooner.

While attempting to highlight the wide spectrum of camp life which Lady Forbes became involved with, he said the following.

> I will give you an example. In the winter of 1914, at the beginning of November 1914, when war work was not the fashion and when the arrangements for the wounded were very far from their present state of perfection, she landed one day at Boulogne, a wet day. She saw the wounded lying in rows on the platform and on the quay the rain was beating on them. They were without shelter and without food. She went back to London that very same day, collected a few stores, made an appeal in the newspapers, and was back again in Boulogne the next morning. She made arrangements with the keeper of the buffet, and that very evening she met the train with the wounded coming in. I think this showed that she was prompt to understand human needs; and from that day, throughout those winter months, through all weathers, all night and all day, sometimes working for twenty-four hours at a stretch, every train that came in was met and the wounded men given drink and food by her and her workers. I venture to say that this was work a great deal more valuable than running the most successful canteen in the world. After that the wounded were treated differently. They were detained at the central station, and that part of the work was taken out of their hands.

It beggars belief what would have become of these men if Lady Forbes and her colleagues had not given of their time and effort to feed and look after them. It is hard to believe that the War Office established a camp the size of the one at Étaples, and did not appear to have given much consideration about how men would be fed, three times a day. It is easy to see how bad feeling would have developed on the part of the men who had to stay at the camp for whatever reason and for however long they had to be there. The harsh living conditions which saw men having to share tents, no matter what the time of year, in addition to their even harsher treatment by the camp instructors and members of the Military Police, would have only been exasperated by their hunger.

What became clear as this discussion continued was the difference in attitude between the 'common man' and those from the upper classes who genuinely cared for them – and those who did not.

> Lady Angela Forbes may go down in the archives of the War Office docketed as a 'camp follower, who kept a canteen at Étaples,' but others will think of her as a woman who was quick to understand and quick to help. A woman who gave all she had to give, her strength and her health, unreservedly to the service of the soldiers. Of this I am sure, that when at last the long drawn out agony of this war is over, when balances are finally adjusted, and when individual efforts in human achievement and human endeavour are seen in their proper proportions, the name of this 'camp follower' will be remembered in many a home in Scotland, in England, and overseas, long after the very existence of those who conspired to blast her reputation and destroy her work has been mercifully forgotten.

Chapter Eleven

James Cullen

Unlike the uncertainty of Percy Toplis's involvement in the Étaples mutiny, there is no such debate or confusion surrounding James Cullen.

Cullen was born on 14 May 1881 in Pollockshaw, Glasgow. He later became a Marine Stoker and actually served for two years in the Royal Navy. When he was 26 years of age, he enlisted in the army on 14 May 1917 at Inverness, when he became Private 20838 in the 3rd Battalion, Argyll & Sutherland Highlanders.

Fortunately, James Cullen's military record has survived. He wasn't a big man in a physical sense, standing at just over 5ft 4in in his stocking feet, with a 34in chest. He had a distinctive Union Jack tattoo inked on his right forearm, which meant that he was easily identifiable. He had married Ida Gray in Bradford on 20 January 1915, but the matrimonial home was at 'Prospect Place', Bolus Lane, Outwood, Wakefield.

It would appear that he must have been conscripted in to the army rather than having joined voluntarily, as his acts of ill-discipline began almost immediately after he had enlisted.

His army service record shows that on 16 July 1917, he was awaiting trial by civilian powers for an assault. He was found guilty and sentenced to seven days' imprisonment. The same record also shows that he served fourteen days detention which began on 27 July 1917, this appears to be connected to a military related matter rather than a civilian one. His 'Regimental Conduct Sheet' shows the following disciplinary matters recorded against him.

On 29 May 1917, just two weeks after having enlisted, he was charged with being insolent and using obscene language to a commissioned officer. For the insolence he was confined to barracks for seven days, and for the obscene language, he received ninety-six hours detention.

On 30 June 1917, he was absent from his barracks from 12 midnight, until 10.25pm the following day. For this breach of military discipline he was punished by being confined to barracks for seven days.

On 2 July 1917, he escaped from his barracks at around 6pm, and after four days on the run, he was picked up in Edinburgh by Military Police, at 11pm on 6 July 1917. His punishment was 168 hours detention.

On 16 July 1917, maybe showing his true colours, he assaulted a female hawker, an offence for which he was tried in a civil court and sentenced to seven days' imprisonment.

On 17 August 1917, he was arrested for desertion by the Military Police, although I am not clear of the difference between being a deserter and absent from the 'tattoo'.

On 8 November 1918, while stationed at Duddingston, a small village to the east of Edinburgh, he was absent from the time of the 'tattoo' and did not return until 6pm on 13 November 1918. For this offence he was deducted a total of twelve days' pay. Did that teach him a lesson? Apparently not, as just eight days later he did the exact same thing.

On 21 November 1918, he was absent from tattoo and did not return until he was apprehended by civilian Police in Waverley Bay, Edinburgh at about 7.30pm on 2 December 1918. His punishment for this breach of military discipline, was to be confined to barracks for seven days.

An article on Wikipedia describes what the term, 'tattoo' means in a military sense.

> A military tattoo is a performance of music or display of armed forces in general. The term comes from the early 17th century Dutch phrase, 'doe den tap toe' or in English, 'turn of the tap, a signal by drummers or trumpeters to instruct innkeepers near military garrisons to stop serving beer, and for soldiers to return to their barracks'.

Not only was James Cullen definitely at Étaples, but he was one of those who actually took part in the mutiny, and in the aftermath was charged with refusing to obey orders, and using threatening language. In his defence Cullen claimed that he discovered 'a most inflammatory' and 'seditious leaflet' which encouraged the men to lay down their arms and stop the war. This was an example that had already been set by their 'Russian brothers'. Cullen stated that the Bolsheviks knew that British soldiers were not happy being in France, and that it would not take too much for them to rebel or raise up and mutiny against their officers. When the Military Policeman Harry Reeve shot dead one of the Scottish contingent, the 'it would not take too much for them to rebel or raise up' moment had well and truly arrived.

The British authorities were duly concerned that if there was full-scale trouble at Étaples, the likelihood was that soldiers who were not initially involved in the situation would be more likely to get involved on the side of the mutineers than they were to help the Military Police and the camp authorities

James Cullen was put on trial in October 1917, in front of a Field General Court Martial, for his part in the Étaples mutiny, found guilty and sentenced to one year's imprisonment. He never served that sentence because it was suspended, but the punishment for Cullen didn't end there. Rather than being dishonourably discharged from the army, as might have been expected in the circumstances, he was put back in uniform and sent to serve on the Western Front, 'at the first opportunity', possibly in the hope that he might be killed.

He quickly deserted but remained in France, travelling around in an officer's uniform, taking in the sights of Paris and Marseille on the way. Having arrived in Belgium he enlisted in the 5th Battalion, Australian Imperial Force, of the Australian Infantry. In January 1918, he was wounded while fighting with his unit, and initially found himself being treated at No. 26 General Hospital at Étaples. He had sustained a bad wound to his left foot which meant that he would be unable to put his left foot to the ground for up to two months, and not walk on it for a further four months. Because of his wounds, he was sent back to the United Kingdom in August 1918, for further medical treatment and was finally demobilised in February 1919.

Even the decision as to whether Cullen should remain in the army or be discharged was a bone of contention. On 7 January 1919, a letter was sent to the Headquarters of the Scottish Command in Edinburgh from the Infantry Record Office, in Perth.

> The attached Army Forms W.3104, B.120, and B.121 are forwarded for a ruling whether No. S/203838S Pte. James Cullin, Argyll and Sutherland Highlanders should be recalled to the Colours.
>
> He was despatched to the dispersal station by the Officer Commanding, 5th Bn., Argyll & Sutherland Highlanders, and is due for transfer to Class 'Z' Army Reserve on 22.1.19, on completion of his 28 days furlough.

Cullen was also a topic of conversation in the House of Commons on 4 March 1919, after he had been unlawfully arrested. Lieutenant-Colonel Wilfrid Ashley, the Conservative Member of Parliament for Fylde in Lancashire, asked the following question of the Secretary of State for War, Winston Churchill.

> Has your attention been drawn in the case of Private James Cullen, Argyll and Sutherland Highlanders, stationed at Galashiels, who, through an error on the part of his commanding officer, was demobilised, and was afterwards arrested as an absentee and brought before the West Riding magistrate at Wakefield; and whether he will see that this man is not penalised for his commanding officer's mistake.

Winston Churchill, Secretary of State for War, by way of reply, said:

> I am not aware of this occurrence, but will make enquiries into the case, and inform my hon. and gallant Friend of the result as early as possible.

When it came to the Étaples mutiny, James Cullen was the real deal. He was in his element and would have been one of those who was at the very heart of what was taking place. In his own words, Cullen relates his role in the Étaples mutiny:

> I was approached by a prominent Communist agitator, who asked me what part I would take in getting the troops to mutiny. There was a small council of action set up and we set about doing everything possible to get a general rising. The Councils of Action, of which I was one, were giving instructions through under channels. The revolt lasted three days, at the end of which a truce was come to between the General Officer Commanding and the rebel troops. I was one who refused point blank to recognise the truce and carried on with a small band of irresponsibles. Eventually we tried to rush the guard one night, but we were repulsed. I was captured and made a prisoner.

But there was more to James Cullen than just being a mutineer, much more. He went on to become one of the leading figures of the Communist Party of Great Britain.

The Hunger Marches from Glasgow to London in 1932 came about largely because of the efforts and influence of Cullen, a member of the National Unemployed Workers Union who were responsible for organising the protest. The march from Glasgow was part of the 'Great National Hunger March against the Means Test' and involved groups of marchers from eighteen of the nation's most economically depressed areas. The protest's first marchers set off from Glasgow on 26 September 1932, and arrived in London at Hyde Park, one month later on 27 October, where they were met by a crowd that was estimated to be in the region of 100,000.

Cullen also went on to become a senior member of the Social Democratic Industrial Peace Union, and at one time he was also the President of the Gorbals Branch of the National Unemployed Workers' Committee.

James Cullen died in Glasgow on 3 August 1964, when he was 83 years of age. He was survived by his wife Ida.

Chapter Twelve

Corporal Jesse Robert Short

It certain circumstances, a government or a controlling authority require a scapegoat. In layman's terms, this means something has happened that was reasonably 'naughty', and not only does it require rectifying, but it has been deemed necessary to set an example, to deter others from doing the same thing in the future.

In the case of the Étaples mutiny, Corporal 626 Jesse Robert Short, of the 24th Battalion, Northumberland Fusiliers, was deemed suitable, by the military authorities, to be that scapegoat. His offence, that of 'attempted mutiny'.

Having been tried before a Field General Court Martial, he was found guilty and his punishment was to be shot at dawn by a firing squad, with the sentence being carried out at Boulogne on 4 October 1917.

The official documentation in his case showed that he was charged with,

> Endeavouring to persuade persons in His Majesty's Regular Forces, to join in a mutiny in that he at Étaples, on 11 September 1917, endeavoured to persuade a picquet not to listen to their officers but to lay down their arms and go with him, and referring to the officer in command of the Picquet, said to the Picquet, 'you ought to get a rope, tie it round his neck with a stone and throw him in to the river,' or words to that effect.

He pleaded 'not guilty'. Under the heading of, 'Finding, and if guilty, sentence,' it read, 'Guilty. To suffer death by being shot.'

Before the war Corporal Short had been a miner who worked at the Heyworth Colliery and lived with his wife, Dinah, and their two young children, daughters Margaret and Mary, at 11 Parkinson, Street, Felling, Gateshead. He enlisted at the outbreak of the war and was posted to the 26th (3rd Tyneside Irish) Battalion, Northumberland Fusiliers, but transferred to the 24th Battalion, before sailing for France.

He would have served and fought with the Tyneside Irish Brigade at the Battle of the Somme, when they suffered 2,100 casualties on the battle's first day, which included 600 killed. The following year he also saw front line action at Ypres. He would have been at Étaples recuperating and undergoing further training before returning to the Western Front.

At his Field General Court Martial, there were two officers who gave written evidence against him. They were Captain E.F. Wilkinson, of the 8th Battalion, West Yorkshire Regiment and 2nd Lieutenant C.D. Thompson, of the 11th Battalion, West Yorkshire Regiment. Captain Wilkinson's statement read as follows.

> On the afternoon of the 11th. instant, I was in charge of a Picquet of 150 armed and 50 unarmed men on the bridge over the River Canche leading from ÉTAPLES to PARIS-PLAGE. At about 9.15 pm about 80 men marched towards the bridge from ÉTAPLES, some of them armed with sticks and notice boards. The Picquet failed to stop these men from crossing the Bridge.
>
> The accused detached himself from this party and while I was addressing my Picquet and remonstrating with them for failing to stand-fast, the accused started haranguing them. Referring to me he said, 'you want to put a rope round that Bugger's neck, tie a stone to it and throw him into the River,' and he told the men that they should not listen to me. Within a few minutes I was able to get the accused arrested.

The statement of 2nd Lieutenant Charles D. Thomson read as follows.

> On the 11/9/1917, I was one of the Officers with a Picquet on the Bridge over the River Canche leading from ÉTAPLES to PARIS-PLAGE. Between 9 and 10 pm the Accused started interrupting Capt. Wilkinson, who was talking to the Picquet, 'Don't listen to the bloody officer' and told him to come along. Referring to Capt. Wilkinson he said, 'that Buggar ought to have a rope tied round his neck with a stone on it and be chucked into the river.'

Although Corporal Short had the right to cross-examine both or either of the witnesses, he declined to do so.

There were four different types of courts martial. The lowest form was a Regiment Court Martial which was used for lesser offences and for other ranks; it could not be used to try commissioned officers.

A General Regimental Court Martial or District Court Martial. These required seven officers to listen to the evidence and decide on the outcome, if the offence was in the UK, but if it was overseas, then only five officers were required. It had limited jurisdiction and could not try commissioned officers. It could also not hear cases where the death penalty was an option, floggings of more than 150 lashes, or where prison sentences could be awarded of more than two years.

Next was a Field General Court Martial. Only three commissioned officers were needed to hear the evidence. If a death sentence was handed down, the decision had to be a unanimous one by all three officers.

A General Court Martial was the army's highest tribunal and dealt with commissioned officers and the more serious cases involving men from the other ranks.

Chapter Thirteen

Treatment of Labour Companies

There had been rumblings of discontent within the rank and file of the British Army even before the events of September 1917 at Étaples.

It is estimated that 100,000 Chinese males were enrolled into the British Army's Chinese Labour Corps during the First World War. These men had been sent direct from China by the Chinese government with the forlorn hope, and misplaced belief, that such an act of assistance to the Allied war effort would ensure the return of their territories at the end of the war, which at the time were either German controlled colonies or concessions.

It is doubtful that any of these men had the slightest idea what they were letting themselves in for. They were put to work by their British 'masters' who treated them abominably. They worked every day of the week, often for ten or twelve hours at a time.

The work which they undertook was varied, but it had a common theme in that none of it was pleasant. It varied from digging trenches, latrines, repairing roads and railway lines, along with the unloading of munitions and supplies, while some were allocated to work in munitions factories and naval shipyards. It must have been a horrible life. By the time they had finished a long day's work, all they could have had time for was to eat a meal and then go to bed, near to exhaustion from their exertions.

When not working they were not allowed out of their camps, herded in like cattle and prevented from leaving by a combination of armed guards and barbed-wire fences; they were more like prisoners than civilian workers of the British Army. They were not even called by their names, instead it was 'Coolie', and then an allocated number. How uncaring and demeaning.

So with the end of the war, one would have thought that their living conditions and general treatment would have improved greatly. Unfortunately that wasn't the case. Their situation worsened. The work they were then expected to do suddenly became a whole lot worse. Their new role required them start clearing mines. Work they certainly had no prior knowledge of. In essence, they were nothing more than human mine detectors, and if they didn't find any, they certainly found numerous dead bodies or human remains which they then had the task of burying.

When it came to the job of filling in the hundreds of miles of trenches that were strung out across Belgium and France, which had been dug out by both sides, the only saving grace was that by the end of the war, when all of this work began there were more than 80,000 of them.

The way the surviving members of the Chinese Labour Corps were treated by the Allies was simply appalling. How the victors in a war could treat human beings of any creed or colour, but especially those who so greatly helped their cause, is hard to understand. Is it any wonder that these men, no matter what their nationality, decided that enough was enough because they had been pushed too far. They determined that they were no longer prepared or willing to be treated in such a way.

What was more astonishing was that rather than understand, listen, or deal with their grievances in a sympathetic and understanding manner, the British authorities simply dealt with the situation as a mutiny and opened fire on them, killing a number of them in the process.

On 5 September 1917, just fourteen miles away to the north of Étaples, at Boulogne, an incident of mutiny by 1,300 men from the Egyptian Labour Corps took place when they went on strike, refusing to work as instructed and remained in their camp. These men who worked hard for the British, were annoyed because their location was regularly targeted by German artillery bombardments, and the home leave they had been promised by the British, was not so readily available as had been promised. This did not create a happy and contented workforce, quite the opposite.

The following day, while trying to break out of their accommodation and make good their escape, they were shot down by soldiers of the British Army, soldiers who had been sent in by Field Marshal Haig to bring an end to the 'dispute'. Whether he specifically gave them an order to shoot the members of the Egyptian Labour Corps dead is unclear, but that's what they did. It was like a turkey shoot. By the time the firing had stopped, twenty-three of the Egyptians had been killed and a further twenty-four of them had been wounded. The fact that they had to 'break out' indicates that they were being held against their will, more like prisoners than civilians working for the British Army.

The Commonwealth War Graves Commission website records the details of the twenty-four members of the Egyptian Labour Corps who died on 6 September 1917. The first four were buried at the Meerut Military Cemetery, St Martin Les-Boulogne, which is situated in the Pas-de-Calais region of France.

Labourer 1051 Abdella, Soliman Ahmed, 73rd Egyptian Labour Corps.
Labourer 2799 Sudani, Abdel Sid Said, 73rd Egyptian Labour Corps.
Labourer 4473 El Morsi, Ibrahim Mohamed, 78th Egyptian Labour Corps.
Labourer 1571 Ahmed, Hamman Shehata, 73rd Egyptian Labour Corps.
Labourer 12439 Senary, Sayed Mohamed, 78th Egyptian Labour Corps.
Labourer 1576 Kader, Sultan Abdul, 78th Egyptian Labour Corps.
Labourer 2214 Sayed, Tarya Awad El, 73rd Egyptian Labour Corps.
Labourer 1606 Mohamedien, Abdel Al, 73rd Egyptian Labour Corps.
Labourer 2613 Salama, Abdel Mawgood, 73rd Egyptian Labour Corps.
Labourer 1747 Abdalla Hussein, Abdel Salem, 73rd Egyptian Labour Corps.
Labourer 1784 Ismail, Hassen Sheikhon, 73rd Egyptian Labour Corps.
Labourer 2827 Karim, Hjssein Gad El, 73rd Egyptian Labour Corps.
Labourer 3435 Aly, Mohamed Ahmed, 78th Egyptian Labour Corps.
Labourer 1563 Hefedi, Zedan Osman, 73rd Egyptian Labour Corps.
Labourer 1607 Aly, Abdel Rahim, 73rd Egyptian Labour Corps.
Labourer 2813 Yussef, Mohamed Aly, 73rd Egyptian Labourer Corps.

Labourer 1114 Khalil, Mohamed Mahmud, 73rd Egyptian Labour Corps.
Labourer 2792 Armed, Aly Hamza, 73rd Egyptian Labour Corps.
Labourer 1487 Mursi, Hassan Aly, 73rd Egyptian Labour Corps.

The following were buried at the Boulogne Eastern Cemetery, which is situated in the Pas-de-Calais region of France.

Labourer 1038 Beshara, Indarwis, 73rd Egyptian Labour Corps.
Labourer F/4372 Ibrahim, Giladishakir, 73rd Egyptian Labourer Corps.
Labourer 1543 Ibrahim, Soliman Shakir, 73rd Egyptian Labour Corps.
Labourer F/4046 Attia, Husseun Mowad, 73rd Egyptian Labour Corps.

The killing of the members of the Egyptian Labour Corps by British soldiers means asking the question, why were they fired upon and killed? They were not trying to hurt or kill anybody, they were not armed, they were simply trying to escape from the compound where they were, in essence, being held by the British. That was their only offence, yet they were shot down like a pack of dogs. Compare this with the similar incident at Étaples, when more than 1,000 British soldiers broke out from their camp, despite an official order confining them to camp having being issued: none of them were shot or even fired upon.

Later the same day a detachment of 400 men from the Honourable Artillery Company, along with a section from the Machine Gun Corps, armed with several Vickers machine guns, arrived at Étaples. Despite the situation not one single shot was fired. Sadly, where the members of the Egyptian Labour Corps were concerned, this displayed the depth of the institutionalised and accepted level of racism that was apparent at the time, certainly among some members of the senior officer ranks of the British Army, that must also include the men who actually opened fire. The obvious question to ask is, would those same British soldiers have opened fire so willingly on their own colleagues?

On 11 September 1917, four more members of No. 74 Labour Company of the Chinese Labour Corps were shot dead by British forces, with a further fifteen being wounded. In October 1917 a similar incident took place which resulted in five Chinese 'Coolies' being shot dead, and another fourteen wounded. A detachment of the Guards Regiment shot dead four members of No. 21 Labour Company of the Chinese Labour Corps in December 1917, near Calais.

The Commonwealth War Graves Commission website shows that during December 1917, fifty-two members of the Chinese Labour Corps died, but it doesn't record how they died. Of these, forty-one are buried in France, nine in Belgium and two in Canada. These included men from the 45th, 47th 59th, 76th 85th 102nd, 105th, Labour Company's to name but a few.

The fact that the members of the Chinese Labour Corps were civilians didn't save them from the outcomes of strict British Military discipline, and with most of them working close to the front lines, they spent a lot of their time either under enemy gunfire, or having to cower from artillery bombardments exploding all around them.

Reading about these actions by British soldiers is almost unbelievable. How could such an action take place? Two possible reasons come to mind. Firstly, they were not British soldiers, they were foreign, non-white civilian workers. This was at a time when the colour of a man's skin mattered greatly, and was relevant to how he was perceived and treated by the white officer-class of the British Army, as well as some of those who held political positions. Secondly, there was a real fear, both militarily and politically, that any such action of rebellion could be the trigger that not only led to a mutiny on foreign soil, but to a revolution back home in the United Kingdom that could result in the collapse of the monarchy as well as the downfall of a government and a political system that had been in place for centuries.

Because of the way in which members of the Chinese Labour Corps were treated for a large part of the time they were in France, the part they played in the First World War has largely been forgotten, or ignored in a historical sense. But it was the Chinese who had the last laugh, so to speak. It was because of how they were treated by the terms of the Treaty of Versailles which ultimately saw the rise of the Communist Party, which still rules China today.

A check of the Commonwealth War Graves Commission website shows that only two members of the Chinese Labour Corps died on 6 September 1917. One is shown as having been buried at the Ruminghem Chinese Cemetery, which is a distance of some thirty-nine miles from Boulogne, while the other man was buried at Noyelles-sur-Mer Chinese Cemetery, which is forty-five miles from Boulogne. With those distances in mind, it is highly unlikely that either man was one of those shot at Boulogne. The question is, where are those men buried?

In the two years between 1916 and 1918, men working with the Chinese Labour Corps were dissatisfied with their treatment and conditions on a regular basis. On many of these occasions their way of making their feelings known was to 'down tools' and refuse to work. The British military authorities took these as acts of mutiny, and dealt with them accordingly, hence so many reports of Chinese Labour Workers being shot dead and wounded.

Chapter Fourteen

Private S/8428 John Pantling, Royal Army Ordnance Corps

Although the First World War had ended, that didn't mean that soldiers were no longer disgruntled about issues which affected them.

British soldiers were no different to those who fought and served with other fighting nations from both sides, in that they could be rebellious if pushed beyond the pale. As the war drew to a close, so more and more demands were brought to bear on their ever-broadening shoulders, especially as the French Army was, by then, just a mere shade of its former self, having never fully recovered from a combination of withering defeats and a number of well documented mutinies.

Although not about Étaples, this story is relevant to the bigger picture in relation to mutiny and rebellion, because it shows that although matters improved after the troubles of September 1917, the lessons which came out of it appear to have been forgotten relatively quickly.

The incident took place in January 1919, at Calais, and was related to the subject of demobilisation, or in the case of the men involved, the slow speed with which the process was being conducted. This scenario also has to be considered with the knowledge that although the Armistice had been signed in the French town of Redonthes on 11 November 1918, the war didn't officially end until 28 June 1919, with the signing of the Treaty of Versailles between Britain, the Allies and Germany. This meant that the British still needed a functioning and effective army, ready to fight if necessary at a moment's notice.

On 11 November 1918, Britain had a total of 6 million combatant troops, and it had been estimated that 1 million of these were needed for occupation duties throughout Europe, the Middle East, Africa, and India.

The first notable post war 'incident' actually took place in England, at Folkestone in Kent to be precise. On the morning of 3 January 1919, orders had been posted at the army's No. 1 Rest Camp in Folkestone, stating that 2,000 men were to embark for France after that morning's parades. This had not been expected by the men, and it was certainly not appreciated by them. In defiance of the order, not a single man made it to parade. Word quickly spread of their act of defiance, and before lunchtime an estimated group of 10,000 soldiers had marched to Folkestone Town Hall to air their grievances. Eventually they were spoken to by a high ranking British Army officer that no man would be compulsorily sent to France, but by the following morning that promise had turned out to be not true, and had simply been slightly watered-down from its original state. New orders were issued stating that a 'certain quota' of men were needed to be sent to France. All this achieved was to cause more outrage among a large group of already disgruntled soldiers who were still in possession of their own rifles. Their ranks were increased further when other soldiers arrived at Folkestone harbour by train who were also due to return to France on leave. Instead they swelled the number of men from the rest camps in Folkestone who had already rebelled, and together formed an impressive and intimidating number of British soldiers who had refused to comply with their orders to sail to France. These actions were copied in other Kent coastal towns where troops once again refused to carry out the orders of their officers and ready themselves for embarkation to France.

Similar actions took place in and around London, where troops demonstrated at Downing Street, but Prime Minister David Lloyd George refused to greet the men and speak with them or listen to their grievances on the advice of Lord Milner, who at the time was the Secretary of State for War. Instead, the large crowd of rebellious soldiers were addressed by

General Sir William Robertson, who between 1916 and 1918 had held the position of Chief of the Imperial Staff. In some respects he was a strange choice as it was well known that he and David Lloyd George didn't particularly see eye-to-eye with each other. Robertson had threatened to resign in early 1917 when Lloyd George had decided that British troops in France would come under the control of the French Commander-in-Chief Robert Nivelle.

Maybe the choice of Robertson was more to do with his understanding of the men. He remains the only member of the British Army to have ever reached the rank of Field Marshal after having begun his career as a private soldier.

Robertson agreed to the troops' demands for better conditions and informed them that there would be no further drafts sent to Russia. Satisfied that they had been listened to, the troops then returned to their barracks.

It wasn't just in England that similar problems occurred. Just a couple of weeks later at the Val de Lievre camp at Calais, men of the Royal Army Ordnance Corps and Mechanical Transport sections were fed up with the conditions they were living in, a common problem and the cause of numerous similar incidents throughout the war. A meeting had taken place in the camp which was attended by a large number of soldiers, with the ultimate aim of bringing about a mutiny. The men had had enough of bloody war and just wanted to go home to their families; they couldn't understand why the process was taking so long to get them where they wanted to be.

One of those who spoke at the gathering was Private John Pantling of the Royal Army Ordnance Corps. The content of the speech that he gave was deemed by the military authorities as being a 'seditious speech to an assembly of soldiers', which resulted in his arrest. His colleagues, along with other soldiers who had been at the gathering were so enraged by his detention that they made their way on mass to the camp's jail and managed to break Pantling out of custody, such were their numbers. Attempts were made to re-arrest Pantling but they failed. Rather than leaving matters as they were, members of the Military Police decided to arrest the sergeant of the guard with a view to charging him for failing to prevent Pantling's arrest. This seemed an even more ridiculous decision than attempting to re-arrest Pantling, and all it actually achieved was to rile the men even further. A common sense approach to the situation was urgently needed before matters spiralled out of control. The camp's commanding officer, possibly because he understood the gravity of the situation, quickly had the sergeant released without any charges, as well as agreeing not to attempt to have Pantling re-arrested. He also met with the men's nominated representatives so he could find out at first-hand what the men's grievances were. As a result of this meeting, he took certain steps to ensure that there was no repeat of the incident, which including agreeing to make certain concessions to the demands that the men had made.

This is when matters started to seriously get out of hand, because what the camp's officers had seen as a lenient approach by the commanding officer, resulted in them taking matters in to their own hands, and they re-arrested Pantling. The following day the men retaliated in kind against Pantling's re-arrest. Having organised Soldiers' Councils, the decision was taken by those selected to be representatives of the men, not to turn up for that morning's reveille. Word of their actions soon spread, and quickly reached the ears of those at other nearby camps, one of which at nearby Vendreux sent 2,000 of its men to support those at the Val de Lievre camp.

From there, some 4,000 men marched to Battalion headquarters, surrounding the building on their arrival, and then demanded the release of Private Pantling. The following morning saw Pantling released and returned to his colleagues; despite this goodwill gesture by the authorities, the number of soldiers now displaying open disobedience had risen to some 20,000 men. With the assistance of French civilian workers, the movement of all British troops by train in the area had come to a grinding halt. This brought about a certain irony, as it also caused the inability of some 5,000 other British soldiers due to return to the UK, from being able to get home and demobilised, which in turn increased the number of troops who were out on strike.

The British military and political authorities were now faced with a real dilemma, as the longer the situation continued the more likely the threat would lead to an all-out revolution back home, which would have more than likely seen Members of Parliament stripped of their positions and the downfall of the monarchy. This was the reality of what was at stake if the situation from there on in wasn't handled with extreme diplomacy. With this in mind, what course of action did the British authorities take? They sent General Julian Byng and a large number of troops to take control of the situation and end the mutiny. Mistake number one: Byng, whether out of arrogance or ignorance, arrived in Calais ahead of his troops, and found himself confronted by the British mutineers, who quickly relieved him of his car.

Mistake number two: sending in the troops, especially brand new ones, who had little or no experience, most of whom were either in their late teens or early twenties. When they finally arrived at the camp, far from putting down the mutiny, these young men, who had even less desire to be in uniform, actually joined sides with the mutineers. With the soldiers now well and truly in control, their working and living conditions not surprisingly improved. Everything they did was coordinated and went through the strike committee, or to give it it's correct title, The Calais Soldier's and Sailors' Association, which operated on a democratic basis. It soon came to light that one of the reasons for their poor supply of food had come about because some of their officers had been selling it to a local French business man.

The mutineers eventually won many concessions from military authorities, and the mutiny slowly wound down, finally coming to an end on 30 January 1919. The collapse of the Calais mutiny was connected in part to the Clyde Strike which had been running at the same time in Scotland.

The entire affair had been a shock and surprise to the British authorities, who had obviously realised that if the mutiny had carried on much longer, the more likely it was to have spread to include the remaining units of the British Army, which would have ultimately led to a revolution, from which there would have been no coming back.

I believe the arrogance of British politicians and senior military personnel was apparent when they were taken by surprise to discover just how effective, organised and professional the mutineers had been, without any help or assistance from a single British Army officer.

None of the mutineers, even those who had been part of the strike committees, were ever charged with any offence connected to the mutiny, but the authorities had learnt the important lesson that their armies could be defeated from within. It was a wake-up call which meant a change in military discipline, and the need to treat their soldiers by new and more up-to-date standards.

As for Private John Pantling, neither his service or pension records have survived, but in the 'Rolls Index Cards for the British Army in the First World War, I found a John T. Pantling who having first arrived in France on 9 September 1914, had served as a Private (7649) in the Leicestershire Regiment, a Private (6516) in the London Regiment, and a Private (S/8428) in the Army Ordnance Corps. Having checked the Commonwealth War Graves Commission website, I could find nobody of that name who had been killed during the war.

In Closing

There are different theories about Étaples, what really happened there and why. But it is clear to me from everything I have read about the place that there was a long-term festering of anger and annoyance, at the harsh conditions in which men were expected to live, no matter what time of the year it was. The food was not up to much either, and the attitude of the 'instructors' and members of the Military Police beggared belief, especially towards those soldiers who had already served on the front line and seen war and all that it entailed at first hand. This was exasperated because many, if not all, of the instructors and Military Police, had not. As far as the men were concerned, they had just had a nice cosy war tucked away among the sand dunes of Étaples.

Being instructed how to do something by those who had not done it for real themselves was a source of annoyance to many of the men who passed through Étaples. So by the time that the mutiny took place in September 1917, different issues had been boiling under the surface for a very long time. Feelings of resentment by the men had reached fever pitch; it was almost as if they were looking for a reason, an excuse, to take matters to another level. At Étaples, that was the death of Corporal 240120 W B Wood of the 1st/4th Battalion, Gordon Highlanders, shot dead by a Military Policeman.

With Corporal Wood's death the situation worsened greatly, of that there is no doubt. The poor treatment and conditions in which the troops had to live and work, caused the situation to exist in the first place. It was the killing of Corporal Wood that brought it to a head, which in turn led to the subsequent and much needed change in the camp. It also highlighted the British Army's inability to effectively deal with the situation, because it was something they had not foreseen, so they had not planned for it.

But the British military base at Étaples was not just defined by the events of September 1917. A Canadian soldier was shot dead on 16 December 1917, during the shooting of men serving with the Labour Corps. There had been similar events in 1916, December 1918, and as late as January 1919. The problem didn't simply go away, the events just weren't recorded in the same way that many of those who actually witnessed them remember.

The unrest and acts of ill-discipline at Étaples were a massive worry to the authorities, both militarily and politically, because of similar events that were taking place throughout Europe at that time, which led to revolutions, governments being overthrown and Royal dynasties being brought to their knees.

Do I believe everything that took place at Étaples is in the public domain? No, not for second do I believe that, but I do believe that we have learnt as much as we ever going to. The soldiers and other witnesses who were going to come forward are gone, leaving their accounts behind them. The camp's diary has been pored through time and time again, and books, plays, and dramatisations have been written and performed, with different truths being displayed. The only thing that can now possibly add anything else to the argument is if the documents and paperwork of the Haig Enquiry in to the Étaples mutiny should miraculously turn up, which I do not believe will ever happen.

Although much has been written about Étaples, it only gained its reputation because of events which took place over six turbulent days in September 1917, known as the Étaples Mutiny, when elements of the British Army challenged the authority of the British Army's High Command.

By that time British forces had lost 510,210 of their men and the Australians had seen the loss of 38,309 of their men. Canada had not faired much better, with the loss of 36,566, and New Zealand losses were 8,932. It wasn't so much a case of morale being affected, but men had definitely started to become disillusioned with the war because of the large number of men who had been killed, allied with the way the war was being fought in the minds of men who had done their fighting in a different time and who seemed to have no problem with the 'acceptable losses' of large numbers of men.

Men's lives were in the hands of the officers under whose command they came, which to many was a reflection of the society from which they were, in part, fighting to break away. This all came to a head during those six days at Étaples. The poor conditions, the brutal treatment, and the lack of sufficient food added up to a toxic environment, which led to the mutiny. They had simply been pushed too far. It said a lot when men would rather be deployed to the trenches of the Western Front, than spend one day longer than they had to at Étaples.

In rebelling in the way that they did, they made a difference. The demands that they made, including the closing of the Bull Ring; that men be allowed to visit Étaples; that men's pay be increased; adequate food be provided; general conditions be improved; and the Military Police be removed, were all met because the British authorities feared that the mutiny at Étaples would be taken up by all British troops, which was a situation that they could ill afford, and most certainly did not want.

Author Biography

Stephen is a happily retired Police officer having served with Essex Police as a constable for thirty years between 1983 and 2013. He is married to Tanya who is also his best friend.

Both his sons, Luke and Ross, were members of the armed forces, collectively serving five tours of Afghanistan between 2008 and 2013. Both were injured on their first tour. This led to his first book; *Two Sons in a Warzone – Afghanistan: The True Story of a Father's Conflict*, which was published in October 2010.

He also has a teenage daughter, Aimee. Both of his grandfathers served in, and survived, the First World War; one with the Royal Irish Rifles, the other in the Mercantile Navy, while his father was a member of the Royal Army Ordnance Corps during and after the Second World War.

Stephen corroborated with one of his writing partners, Ken Porter, on a previous book published in August 2012, *German POW Camp 266 – Langdon Hills*. It spent six weeks as the number one bestselling book in Waterstones, Basildon between March and April 2013. They have also collaborated on four books in the 'Towns & Cities in the Great War' series by Pen and Sword. Stephen has also written other titles for the same series of books, and In February 2017 his book, *The Surrender of Singapore – Three Years of Hell 1942–45*, was published. This was followed in March 2018 by *Against All Odds: Walter Tull the Black Lieutenant*. October 2018 saw the publication of *Animals in the Great War,* and in January 2019, *A History of the Royal Hospital Chelsea – 1682-2017 – The Warriors Repose*. These last two books were written with his wife, Tanya.

Stephen has co-written three crime thrillers which were published between 2010 and 2012, and centre round a fictional detective, named Terry Danvers.

When he is not writing, Tanya and he enjoy the simplicity of going out for a coffee, and walking their four German Shepherd dogs early each morning, while most sensible people are still fast asleep in their beds.

Sources

www.parliament.uk
www.wikipedia.org
www.cwgc.co.uk
www.nationalarchives.gov
www.cwgc.org
www.ancestry.co.uk
www.militarian.com
www.warpoets.org.uk
www.hac.org.uk
www.wartimememoriesproject.com
www.themenbehindthemedals.com
www.britishnewspaperarchive.co.uk
www.libcom.org
www.marxist.com

Index